8,95

ECONOMIC ISSUES IN
METROPOLITAN GROWTH

Economic Issues in Metropolitan Growth EDITED BY

PAUL R. PORTNEY

Papers Presented at a Forum

Conducted by Resources for the Future

May 28–29, 1975, in Washington, D.C.

PUBLISHED FOR RESOURCES FOR THE FUTURE
BY THE JOHNS HOPKINS UNIVERSITY PRESS
BALTIMORE AND LONDON

Copyright © 1976 by The Johns Hopkins University Press
Manufactured in the United States of America

Library of Congress Catalog Card Number 76-15906

ISBN 0-8018-1885-0

Resources for the Future is a nonprofit organization for research and education in the development, conservation, and use of natural resources and the improvement of the quality of the environment. It was established in 1952 with the cooperation of the Ford Foundation. Part of the work of Resources for the Future is carried out by its resident staff; part is supported by grants to universities and other nonprofit organizations. Unless otherwise stated, interpretations and conclusions in RFF publications are those of the authors; the organization takes responsibility for the selection of significant subjects for study, the competence of the researchers, and their freedom of inquiry.

This book is one of RFF's studies on institutions and public decisions, which are prepared under the direction of Clifford S. Russell. It was supported by a grant from the Edna McConnell Clark Foundation. Paul R. Portney is the assistant director of RFF's Institutions and Public Decisions Division.

The figures for this book were drawn by Federal Graphics. The manuscript was edited by Jo Hinkel.

RFF editors: Herbert C. Morton, Joan R. Tron, Ruth B. Haas, Jo Hinkel, and Sally A. Skillings

Contents

Preface

DURING THE SUMMER OF 1973, Resources for the Future applied to the Edna McConnell Clark Foundation for a grant to extend its research in the area of "government structure and process as they relate to environmental quality, resources use, and economic growth." This area of research had come to be explored at RFF because of the strong feeling of Allen V. Kneese and Edwin T. Haefele (at that time directors of the Quality of the Environment and Regional and Urban Studies programs, respectively) that misunderstandings about the way collective choices were actually made lay at the heart of many environmental and urban problems. These feelings had led to a modest research effort at RFF in the area of collective decision making in the several years previous to the grant application. From this research came the attempt by Haefele, Clifford S. Russell, and Walter O. Spofford to introduce political constraints—in addition to the more familiar technological and economic constraints—into their comprehensive model of residuals management in the Delaware River Basin. These efforts were expanded subsequent to the Clark Foundation award of a three-year $300,000 grant.

The first and partial product of that grant was *The Governance of Common Property Resources,* edited by Haefele and published by RFF late in 1974. The papers in that volume dealt with the political, economic, and legal problems which attend resources that are publicly owned and managed (and subject, therefore, to a variety of competing claims for their use) or those which are not owned at all. The scope of the papers was wide, ranging from the management of wilderness lands and natural park areas to the legitimacy of producers groups in the political and legislative processes.

This volume, the second produced under the Clark grant, focuses on the problems of metropolitan areas, thereby extending yet narrowing the earlier work. This focus was chosen for two reasons: first, although

ix

only 1 percent of the land area in the continental United States was urbanized in 1970, more than 73 percent of the population inhabited such areas; second, problems of governance and governmental finance, while not the exclusive province of urban areas, are certainly most pronounced there. The woes of New York City and by extension, of New York State, have become the most visible, of course. Municipal bankruptcy or large-scale default on the city's short-term bond obligations became a distinct possibility a few months after a conference was held at which the chapters in this volume were presented. This conference brought together economists, other academics, and members of what we refer to as the "real world"—builders, planners, politicians, lawyers, and environmentalists. Their discussions of and reactions to the presentations were lively, sometimes heated, and always interesting. It is hoped that the chapters in this volume communicate to the reader both the controversiality and the importance of these issues.

January 1976   PAUL R. PORTNEY
                                                         Washington, D.C.

ECONOMIC ISSUES IN
METROPOLITAN GROWTH

1 / PAUL R. PORTNEY

Introduction

MANY OF THE PROBLEMS of central cities are conventionally ascribed to the flight of moderate- and upper-income households to suburban jurisdictions. As even the casual observer of current events can recite, this has resulted in a declining tax base in central cities during a period when the service demands of their remaining, poorer residents have increased sharply. In addition, this migration from central cities to suburban jurisdictions has caused considerable problems for the suburbs as well. These suburban problems have centered around questions of growth—Whether to grow? How much to grow and when? How to shut off growth when enough has taken place?

Because the fact of suburban growth, often at the expense of the central city fisc, affects both kinds of jurisdictions in metropolitan areas, it was a natural topic on which to focus our research. That this was a relevant choice seems indisputable—the current debates in district and appeals courts as well as in the Supreme Court over the constitutionality of growth-control mechanisms, the reintroduction in the Congress of a National Land Use Planning Act (1975), and the debates within local governments over the financing of growth-induced changes in public service demands all attest to the timeliness of the growth, governance, and finance issues.

The chapters in this volume are addressed to these related issues; they reflect the authors' belief that economic analysis, even in the abstract, can make important contributions to the understanding of metropolitan growth problems. In addition, while not all the chapters deal explicitly with improvements in public decision making, such implications are

The author is affiliated with Resources for the Future.

1

never far beneath the surface. In order to understand these implications, however, it is necessary to be clear about whether the stance taken by each author is prescriptive or descriptive. In fact, certain sections of each chapter describe and analyze existing aspects of the growth, governance, and finance nexus. But most chapters also contain explicit prescriptions; that is, given some basis for making value judgments, the author's purpose is to detail what ought or ought not be done with respect to some problem. In addition, what we might call a hypothetical approach is taken by several authors who describe what would happen if a particular policy were followed. To minimize confusion about the purpose of each paper, I will summarize in the following paragraphs the approach taken by each author, drawing attention as well to the implications which each chapter has for improved collective decision making in the metropolitan area.

In chapter 2 Tara Ellman discusses the fiscal impact study, a kind of financial analysis employed by local governments in assessing the expected effects of proposed development. Her primary intention is to describe the nature of these studies, particularly the concept of the "break-even line," to discuss the ways in which the studies are being used and could be used, and to detail the possible effects of such uses of fiscal impact studies. In so doing, she first makes a specific and fairly typical set of assumptions about the revenues derived from, and the expenditures necessitated by, the addition of several types of households to each of nine local jurisdictions in the Washington, D.C., SMSA (standard metropolitan statistical area). Using these estimates, she shows how each community would view as a potential new resident each type of household based on a fiscal impact study. That is, Ellman presents estimates of the fiscal "deficit" or "surplus" which each community would attribute to a new home inhabited by each type of household. She then shows the uses which local governments might make of such information in passing on the acceptability of new development.

Later, she discusses the effects which the various kinds of intergovernmental transfers are likely to have on the results of fiscal impact studies. Of particular interest is her discussion of the sometimes unintended effects of these grants. Ellman concludes with suggestions for ways in which communities can, through the use of fiscal impact studies, protect the interests of existing residents while, at the same time, at least partially mitigating the exclusionary effects with which courts at all levels have found fault.

These fiscal impact studies play an important role in local governments' decisions about the acceptability of growth. Therefore, Ellman's paper is useful in that it explains one way in which residents' preferences for or against growth are translated into their community's "growth policy." Fiscal impact studies are, it would seem, one way of obviating the need for communitywide referenda on the many proposed developments which any community might face.

In chapter 3, Jon C. Sontelie and I focus on the local public services which a community provides to its residents. But rather than analyzing the way in which these services are currently provided, we suggest a very different alternative. Specifically, we consider the question, What would happen should a community's public service supply decisions be designed to maximize the value of the residential property within its boundaries?

This question comes out of our recognition that many, perhaps most, of the locally provided public services (including education, police and fire protection, sanitation, etc.) are also provided in one form or another by private firms. Since private firms are ostensibly run for profit, and, as we argue, the "profits" arising from a community's supply decisions accrue to property owners, it seems natural to examine the implication of profit maximization (in the form of property value maximization) if practiced by local communities. Using a strong set of assumptions about the housing market in large metropolitan areas, we show that property value-maximizing supply decisions by local governments, when coupled with utility-maximizing residential decisions by households, result in an efficient allocation of resources to the provision of local public goods.

Since the concept of allocative efficiency is dear to the hearts of most economists, our proof may appear to have both prescriptive as well as descriptive importance. That is, if efficiency is a goal toward which one believes governments should strive, it would appear that local governments *ought* to make supply decisions according to the property value-maximizing criterion. Because of the controversial nature of this normative conclusion, we devote considerable attention to factors which would tend to vitiate it. We note the strong nature of the assumptions underlying our analysis and especially acknowledge the high value that residents may attach to their own neighborhoods and the friendships they have developed—attachments that serve to limit the mobility which we ascribe to households and which is central to our conclusions. We also consider the effects of interjurisdictional spillovers and the potentially adverse distributional consequences of property value maximization.

Finally, we suggest a way of financing proposed changes in the levels of the public services provided by any community. Our scheme, which would distribute the total cost of such changes among property owners in proportion to the benefits they could be expected to receive, would result in unanimous voter approval or rejection of proposed changes. Given the great conflicts which arise under the current system of effecting such changes in public services—that is, individual voting in popular referenda—our proposal would seem to merit close attention.

Mark F. Sharefkin, in chapter 4, focuses attention on the changing nature of the debate over the public utilities—electricity, water and sewers, and public transportation. These services are currently coming under close scrutiny because of the "energy crisis," by which is meant increases in the price of oil, electricity, and natural gas; because of the environmental effects of the siting and operation of utility facilities; and because of the role played by these services in the location and timing of growth in metropolitan (as well as rural) areas. Sharefkin notes that the attention being paid to these environmental and growth problems marks a departure from the previous, almost single-minded concern with efficient provision of the public utility services.

Sharefkin begins by summarizing the rationale behind the public regulation of the three services he considers. He then describes the particular characteristics of each of the services and, in considerable detail, the way in which pricing and capital investment decisions are currently made in each. This information is essential to the understanding of the effects of these services on urban and suburban growth. The topics discussed include the peak-load pricing of both electricity and transportation.

Popular explanations for the irrationality of pricing and investment policies in the public utilities are then considered by Sharefkin, who pays particular attention to the nature of the bodies regulating these utilities. The perverse policies with which economists have long been concerned turn out to be understandable if one views regulatory commissions as (1) acting to maximize their size or influence, or both; and (2) acting as buffers between competing interest groups.

Finally, Sharefkin proposes a better way of making public utility (especially electricity) pricing and investment decisions in the metropolitan area. This would involve the formation of a metropolitan areawide government, which would then charter regulatory commissions (now chartered by state governments). The metropolitan government, rather than the commissions, would be responsible for investment decisions, and this would, he argues, force conflicts between interest groups to be resolved by elected representatives rather than by appointed commissioners. Given that this would vest considerable power in the metropolitanwide government and alter the present configuration of local governments, the implications of his suggestions for collective decision making are obvious.

In chapter 5, Barry Schechter covers the fiscal impact or new development fees (or taxes), which Ellman touches upon in chapter 2. Whereas Ellman merely introduces the possibility that developers be taxed by the communities in which they build, Schechter goes much further. He first presents and evaluates the arguments advanced in behalf of such fees or taxes by considering two primary arguments: first, that such fees are needed to protect existing residents from the "fiscal externalities" visited upon them in certain instances by new residents; and second, that such fees can be used to correct the environmental damage (for example, increased air or water pollution) or visual blight which new development might bring. In this discussion, he focuses on the inter- and intragovernmental subsidies characterizing the federal system; he also pays particular attention to the inefficiencies inherent in the free market for development, considering whether efficiency gains might result from a development tax.

Next, Schechter turns his attention to a quite important but often misunderstood aspect of the development tax: what effect it has on the price and supply of housing. Whereas it has been asserted, most often by builders, that a tax on new development would merely be shifted forward to the purchasers of new homes, Schechter argues otherwise. He claims that the development tax would, in fact, be borne by all tenants in the area, while those benefiting from the tax would be landowners. Thus, while we might at first expect existing residents, both renters and owners alike, to line up against potential immigrants with respect to such a development tax, the battle lines should apparently be drawn up quite differently.

Schechter's analysis is interesting for a number of reasons, not the least of which is that it points out the danger of jumping to conclusions about likely political coalitions. For if his analysis is correct, and if renters both within and outside the community considering such a tax were economically sophisticated, they would line up with those opposing such a tax despite the likely claims of proponents that renters, by favoring a new development tax, would be protecting themselves from congested facilities or other diminutions in public services. In short, it would be in the interest of all metropolitan residents to carefully think through the effects of such taxes. Thus, Schechter's chapter, like Ellman's, sheds light on the decision of local residents to control growth not through individual referenda, but rather through a kind of automatic mechanism— a mechanism, it seems, that may not be in the interests of those citizens who often approve it.

J. Michael Cummins, in chapter 6, discusses the provision of public goods by private, regulated firms, including the utilities. The increasing frequency of this phenomenon, which Cummins documents, is on its face puzzling: why would a private firm provide, free of charge, services which are normally the domain of the government? Cummins answers this question by pointing out that such behavior may be but a sophisticated extension of profit maximization. This will be so if, in exchange for the public good or service it provides, the firm is allowed a relaxation in the regulatory constraint under which it must operate. A regulatory commission that permitted such a relaxation would, therefore, be acting as a buffer between the citizen–consumers and the regulated firm.

Given that this practice may be taking place, Cummins's concern is primarily with its economic implications. That is, can we expect regulated firms to provide efficient levels of the public goods and services they choose and, if so, under what conditions? To analyze these questions, he develops a simple model of the regulated firm which, contrary to most analyses, takes its regulatory constraint as endogenous rather than exogenous to its operation. The firm is compensated for its provision of public goods through allowable increases in the price of the private product it sells; in other words, "excise taxes" are levied on the latter to finance the former. Cummins shows that under certain extremely restrictive conditions private, regulated firms can efficiently provide such public goods. And, he argues, given the likely existence of other distortions in the economy, one cannot even be sure that the imposition of an excise tax is suboptimal.

According to Cummins, the palatability of the kind of *quid pro quo* arrangement which he describes must be judged on grounds other than

mere efficiency. As regards the distributional consequences of the private provision of public goods, he makes an interesting point: if regulated firms can discriminate on the basis of price, it may be possible for
them to provide certain public goods with favorable distributional consequences. The possibility also exists for competition between private
firms for the right to provide certain public services.

In conclusion, it is interesting to note that these papers on urban
growth all turn out, unintentionally, to deal with one or another form of
market failure: Cummins's and Sharefkin's with decreasing-cost industries, Schechter's and Ellman's with technological and pecuniary externalities, and Sonstelie's and mine with public goods. Perhaps this
should serve once again to demonstrate the frailty of the competitive
model as a guide to public policy. Moreover, the difficulty with which
varieties of market failure are corrected, even in theoretical models,
makes it all too clear that practical solutions to urban growth problems
will not soon be forthcoming. The chapters which follow are offered,
then, as a beginning.

2 / TARA ELLMAN

Fiscal Impact Studies in a
Metropolitan Context

IN SIMPLE TERMS, a fiscal impact study is one that compares the revenue
which a local government expects to receive from any particular land
use against the cost to the local government of providing public services
to that land use. Although a trickle of these studies has issued from local
governments, developers, and researchers for decades,[1] this flow has increased to flood proportions in the last few years.[2] The fiscal problems
of some local governments, the resistance of local taxpayers to tax increases, and a general trend toward increased public regulation of land
use have motivated local governments to scrutinize the fiscal consequences of development more carefully than ever before. Concurrently,
improvements in the methodology of fiscal impact studies have enabled
them to do so. The Department of Housing and Urban Development
(HUD), for example, has sponsored a manual enabling local governments with limited resources to do fiscal impact studies,[3] and computer
programs developed by private companies, local governments, and

The author, formerly at Resources for the Future, is a private consultant in
Berkeley, California.
[1] For a good discussion of the literature from 1933–60, see Ruth L. Mace,
Municipal Cost-Revenue Research in the United States (Chapel Hill, N.C.,
Institute of Government, University of North Carolina, 1961).

[2] The most extensive recent bibliography, cross-referenced and annotated, is
Real Estate Research Corporation, *The Costs of Sprawl, Literature Review and
Bibliography* (Washington, D.C., Govt. Print. Off., 1974).

[3] Connecticut Development Group, Inc., *Cost-Revenue Impact Analysis for
Residential Developments* (Springfield, Va., National Technical Information
Service, 1974) PB239214/AS.

others have made possible the mass production of such studies.[4] If the present trend continues, fiscal impact studies will soon be a customary part of land development proposals in many places.

Although some fiscal impact studies may be used to project future budgets or to plan capital improvement programs, the purpose of most is to provide information about the fiscal effects of existing or proposed developments; they may focus on an entire jurisdiction, a geographic portion thereof, a type of development, or a single development. Many fiscal impact studies deal with specific residential development proposals which are of particular concern to local governments because, unlike industrial and commercial developments, residential land uses often generate more expenditures than revenues.

This chapter analyzes the consequences, should many local governments within a metropolitan area use the most common type of fiscal impact study to screen residential development proposals, rejecting those which failed to meet an established fiscal standard. Although apparently only isolated examples of local governments using fiscal impact studies as screening mechanisms exist, the studies are easily applied to this purpose. Moreover, this use may become increasingly attractive to local officials grappling with fiscal problems. While the extensive use of fiscal impact studies discussed here is not now a reality, it could become so.

In the following section, I will discuss the mechanics of the most common type of fiscal impact study for residential development. Later, I will deal both with the possible decisions which local governments could make based on their studies and with the effects that these decisions would have on current and potential residents of a jurisdiction. Intergovernmental transfers and the division of financial responsibility for some public services between state and local governments, both of which affect the conclusions of fiscal impact studies, will also be discussed. Finally, I will suggest ways for a state government to moderate

[4] The city of San Diego, Calif., has developed such a computer program. For a description of others, see Dennis E. Gale, *The Municipal Impact Evaluation System: Computer Assisted Cost-Revenue Analysis of Urban Development* (Chicago, American Society of Planning Officials, September 1973).

Anthony Pellegrini, *A Model for Multiple Criteria Analysis of Land Use Plans* (Springfield, Va.: National Technical Information Service, December 1972) PB221916.

Gerald C. Sumner and Annette W. Bonner, *Design for an Urban Service Resource/Cost Model* (Santa Monica, Calif., Rand, June 1973).

some of the undesirable consequences which might result from the local governments' use of fiscal impact studies.

THE DETERMINANTS OF FISCAL IMPACT

Methodology

In the usual terminology, if the cost of providing services to a particular household exceeds the revenue which a local government expects to receive from it, the household is said to cause a "deficit;" in the opposite case, the household is said to produce a "profit" for the local government.[5] A standard methodology for the determination of these expected costs and revenues does not exist. However, in most studies of specific developments prepared by local governments or developers the same general approach is used. To estimate the expected costs to a local government caused by an additional household, the number of "need units" which the household would generate must first be determined. Need units are any appropriate indicator of the household's demand for local government services, such as the number of persons or students. Multiplying the total number of need units by the annual operating cost per need unit for each type of service yields total annual operating costs of the household to the community. Most studies use the current average cost per user for each service to estimate future costs, but cost estimates are sometimes obtained directly from the staff of the local government.[6] To calculate the total annual cost, annualized capital costs are frequently added to operating costs.

Revenues generated by an additional household are estimated by applying the current nominal or effective tax rate of the local government to the estimated taxable resources of the household. Although assessed value of real property is generally the most important local tax

---

[5] The designation *household,* as used throughout this chapter, includes the occupants of a dwelling unit as well as the dwelling, and its land and accessories. Since fiscal impact studies generally deal with groups of households, the designation also refers to a typical household with the average characteristics of a group.

[6] The manual prepared for HUD by the Connecticut Development Group (see footnote 3, p. 8) is basically a set of questions designed to elicit careful cost estimates from a local government's staff members. The author argues that the results of this approach are more accurate than using averages, as is done in most cases.

resource contributed by households, income, personal property, or consumption may be important in some communities.

Obviously, the estimation of a local government's costs, its effective tax rates, and the socioeconomic characteristics of the future inhabitants of a proposed dwelling presents serious problems, which will not be discussed here.[7] In the following section it is assumed that local governments use fiscal impact studies of the general type described above. Whether such studies yield reliable conclusions does not affect the discussion.

Break-even Lines
The "desirability" of a household with specified need units and tax resources depends on the local government's tax rate and its cost per need unit. This becomes apparent if we consider a simple case under the following assumptions:

1. The local government balances its budget.
2. All its revenue comes from one local tax resource—say, the assessed value of real property.
3. It provides one service—say, education—for all existing or additional students at a constant marginal cost per student.
4. The appropriate indicator of the local government's wealth is the ratio of the total tax resource units to the total need units in the jurisdiction—in this example, the assessed value per student.

Under these assumptions, a local government with N dollars of assessed value per student must set its tax rate so that the revenue from N dollars of assessed value equals the cost per student. Obviously, the local government would "break even"—that is, its cost of educating a student would exactly equal the tax revenue generated by a household—on a one-student household with N dollars of assessed value, on a two-student household with $2N$ dollars of assessed value, and, in general, on any household with N dollars of assessed value per student. All households for which the local government would break even could be represented by points on a graph showing assessed value per student on the vertical axis and students per household on the horizontal axis.

---

[7] For a discussion of methodology, see Thomas Muller, *Fiscal Impacts of Land Development: A Critique of Methods and Review of Issues* (Washington, D.C., Urban Institute, 1975).

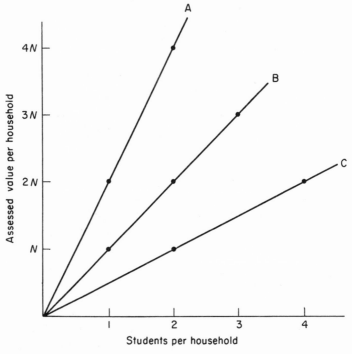

Fig. 2-1.   Break-even lines for three hypothetical communities.

When joined, these points form a line, hereafter termed a *break-even line,* which has a slope equal to the wealth (that is, the assessed value per student) of the local government. For example, in figure 2-1, jurisdiction B has N dollars of assessed value per student and all households for which it breaks even have N dollars of assessed value per student; its break-even line has a slope of N. All households in community B with a larger ratio of assessed value to students would produce a profit for the local government (represented by points above and to the left of jurisdiction B's break-even line), while those with less assessed value per student would cause a deficit (represented by points under the line).

A break-even line could be drawn for each of the local governments in a metropolitan area. Each line would have a slope equal to its wealth as measured by the assessed value per student. Plotted on the same graph, they would form an array of lines ordered by the relative wealth of the jurisdictions, with the richest having the highest and steepest break-even line and the poorest jurisdiction the lowest and flattest line.

Tax Rates

Assuming that the jurisdiction balances its budget, the ratio of expenditures per student to the tax rate in each jurisdiction must equal its wealth, as given by the assessed value per student. Consequently, for a given cost per student the tax rate is always lower in a rich community than in a poor one. Of course, a rich jurisdiction with very high expenditures per student can have a higher absolute tax rate than a poor jurisdiction which chooses to spend less per student, but the residents of the rich community always pay a lower tax rate for what they get. This simple fact explains why any household with a given number of need units has to own more tax resources to pay its way in a rich community than in a poor one.

To keep the ratio of resource to need units equal to the ratio of the costs per need unit to the tax rate (which is necessary to balance the budget), any time the local government changes its expenditure per student it must also change the tax rate proportionately. Therefore, increasing the cost per student would not affect the break-even line.

Break-even Lines for Existing Versus New Households

In this simplified case, the assumption that the marginal cost of educating an additional student is equal to the average cost makes the break-even lines the same for both groups. If one assumes, as is sometimes done in fiscal impact studies, that marginal costs for services are not equal to average costs, the break-even lines will be different. In existing communities the ratio of the cost per need unit to the tax rate has to be constant (at a given wealth) in order to balance the jurisdiction's budget. In studies of new developments, however, only the tax rate is assumed constant. Consequently, if higher than average costs per need unit are attributed to new households, these households must own more assessed value in order to cover the additional costs. This means their break-even line is higher than that for the whole community.

In practice this distinction is not very important since most fiscal impact studies are based on the convenient assumption that, at least for operating costs, marginal costs equal average costs. Economies or diseconomies of scale in operating costs are seldom assumed. However, higher than average capital costs are frequently attributed to new households and, consequently, break-even lines for new households tend to be somewhat higher than those for existing households.

Changes Over Time

Since the break-even line is determined basically by the local government's wealth, it shifts upward as the jurisdiction becomes wealthier. This would happen, for example, when a profitable household or a profitable nonresidential development enters the community. Of course, the break-even line shifts downward as the jurisdiction becomes poorer.

The fiscal impact of particular households could change over time as a consequence of the jurisdiction's land use policies. A local government which increases its wealth by admitting only profitable households, for example, would find that some originally profitable households would no longer be so because of the increased wealth of the community as a whole. Also, emigration of households out of the community or changes in the wealth or service consumption of those remaining could alter the ratio of total resource units to need units, even in a community without new entrants.

Most fiscal impact studies cover a short period during which all variables, except the number of new households and related developments, are assumed constant. A few studies consider changes in the fiscal impact of a proposed residential development over time because (1) the costs per need unit may change, or (2) the ratio of resource units to need units of new households may change. However, few studies, if any, consider the change in fiscal impact resulting from changes in the wealth of the jurisdiction.

An Example of Break-even Lines of Nine Suburban Communities

In this section I will discuss what nine local governments—the suburban jurisdictions of the Washington, D.C., standard metropolitan statistical area (SMSA)—would have concluded in 1972 had they done fiscal impact studies of the same hypothetical households using the same, relatively simple methodology. My purpose here is to show realistic examples of break-even lines, to illustrate some of the other characteristics of fiscal impact studies, and to suggest some of the consequences were a group of local governments to use the results of fiscal impact studies to guide their land use decisions.

A complete explanation of the methodology used here is contained in the Appendix (see page 38). Briefly, a relatively simple version of the "average cost" methodology is used, in which it is assumed that the marginal cost of new residents to a local government is equal to the current total expenditures for services to existing residents divided by the current number of users of each service. A typical assumption, as I have pointed out, is that the cost of an additional student is equal to the current average cost per student.

In order to make "tax resource units," "need units," and "wealth" precisely defined concepts, it is necessary to assume that local governments obtain all revenue from a single tax resource and provide a single service at a uniform cost per user. Obviously, in a fiscal impact study of a complex, real community approximate indicators of tax resources, service demand, and wealth must suffice. Since average costs of education are high and account for a substantial portion of the expenditures of most suburban jurisdictions, the number of students is generally a useful indicator of a household's demand for service. Assessed property value or household income generally can be used as approximate indicators of tax resources.

Household income is used here as the basic tax resource unit, although a specific median house value is assumed for each of the six income categories. Fiscal impact studies often assume some fixed relationship between the value of a dwelling and the income of its occupants, usually based on U.S. Census data, since in most communities some revenues are based on assessed value and others are income related. In this case, the property value figures are the median values of recently purchased, owner-occupied homes by income class for the United States.[8]

Public school students are used as a measure of need units, since education is the most important service of these jurisdictions; in 1972 it accounted for between 38 and 68 percent of their total operating expenditures, with costs per student ranging from approximately $800 to $1,500.[9]

Figure 2-2 shows the results of fiscal impact studies for eighteen hypothetical household types for nine local governments. The heavy lines indicate the approximate break-even lines. The numbers in the cells are estimates (in hundreds of dollars) of the amount of the "profit" or "deficit" which the community would attribute to various household types. Those households shown above and to the left of the break-even lines are profitable, while those indicated below and to the right cause deficits.

    [8] U.S. Bureau of the Census, *Census of Housing 1970. Residential Finance* (Washington, D.C., Govt. Print. Off., 1973) vol. 5, p. 127.
    [9] U.S. Bureau of the Census, *Census of Governments, 1972, Local Government in Metropolitan Areas* (Washington, D.C., Govt. Print. Off., 1974) vol. 5, pp. 271–273.

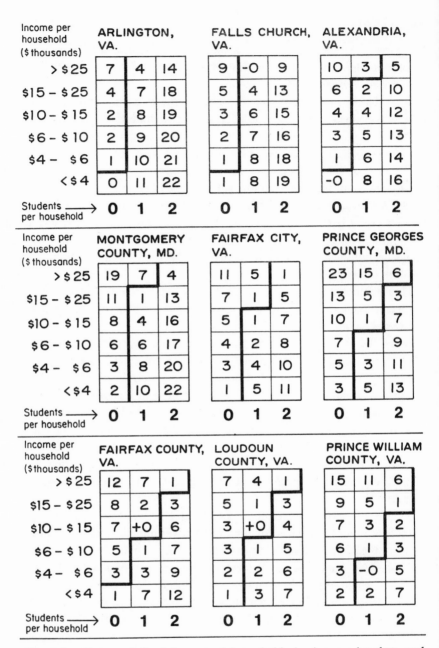

Fig. 2-2. Estimated fiscal impact of households by income brackets and number of students. Figures above and to the left of the heavy lines are estimated fiscal profits per households in hundreds of dollars. Figures below and to the right of the heavy lines are estimated deficits in hundreds of dollars.

There is no satisfactory wealth indicator for ranking these nine jurisdictions, as they vary considerably in tax structures, land use characteristics, population characteristics, types of services provided, and other factors which would affect our choice. Although they rely on the property tax for between 52 and 70 percent of their revenue from local sources, each has income-related taxes such as sales or utility consumption taxes. The two counties in Maryland derive substantial revenues from income taxes.[10] Consequently, market value of real property per student and per capita and personal income per student and per capita are all reasonable wealth indicators in these jurisdictions. Unfortunately, these indicators produce different wealth rankings, as is shown in table 2-1. However, Arlington County and the city of Falls Church, Virginia, which were ranked third or higher by all four indicators, are clearly relatively rich. The relatively poor members of the group appear to be Prince Georges, Prince William, and Loudoun counties, which ranked sixth or lower by all four indicators, and probably Fairfax County, which ranked sixth or lower by three indicators. With the qualification that this ranking may be approximate, the tables in figure 2-2 are ordered, reading across columns, from richest to poorest, using personal income per student as the wealth indicator.

Figure 2-2 shows clearly that the richer jurisdictions have higher break-even lines and, therefore, find fewer categories of households profitable than the poorer jurisdictions. Of the eighteen hypothetical types we considered, the number of household types which would be profitable is listed below:

Rank by personal income per student	*Profitable household types*	
1. Arlington County, Va.	5	relatively rich
2. Falls Church, Va.	5	
3. Alexandria, Va.	6	
4. Montgomery County, Md.	7	
5. Fairfax City, Va.	8	
6. Prince Georges County, Md.	10	relatively poor
7. Fairfax County, Va.	9	
8. Loudoun County, Va.	10	
9. Prince William County, Va.	12	

[10] Ibid. Additional data may be found in Maryland Comptroller of the Treasury, Income Tax Division, *Summary Report, Individual Income Tax Returns Filed for the Year 1972* (Annapolis, March 1974).

TABLE 2-1. Wealth Indicators for Suburban Jurisdictions in the Washington, D.C., SMSA, for 1972

Personal income per student

Rank	Jurisdiction	Personal income per student
1	Arlington County, Va.	$59,000
2	Falls Church, Va.	57,600
3	Alexandria, Va.	45,800
4	Montgomery County, Md.	34,100
5	Fairfax City, Va.	24,900
6	Prince Georges County, Md.	22,600
7	Fairfax County, Va.	22,300
8	Loudoun County, Va.	20,100
9	Prince William County, Va.	17,900

Personal income per capita

Rank	Jurisdiction	Personal income per capita
1	Falls Church, Va.	$9,800
2	Montgomery County, Md.	7,800
3	Arlington County, Va.	7,500
4	Alexandria, Va.	6,300
5	Fairfax City, Va.	6,200
6	Fairfax County, Va.	5,800
7	Prince Georges County, Md.	5,400
8	Loudoun County, Va.	4,900
9	Prince William County, Va.	4,400

Market value of taxable real property per student

Rank	Jurisdiction	Market value per student
1	Arlington County, Va.	$112,000
2	Falls Church, Va.	99,100
3	Alexandria, Va.	78,500
4	Montgomery County, Md.	57,400
5	Fairfax City, Va.	51,600
6	Loudoun County, Va.	49,200
7	Fairfax County, Va.	46,100
8	Prince William County, Va.	40,300
9	Prince Georges County, Md.	35,500

Market value of taxable real property per capita

Rank	Jurisdiction	Market value per capita
1	Falls Church, Va.	$17,100
2	Arlington, Va.	14,300
3	Fairfax City, Va.	12,800
4	Montgomery County, Md.	12,200
5	Fairfax County, Va.	12,200
6	Loudoun County, Va.	11,700
7	Alexandria, Va.	10,700
8	Prince William County, Va.	9,900
9	Prince Georges County, Md.	7,800

Sources:: Statistics on estimated personal income by place of residence are from the U.S. Department of Commerce, *Survey of Current Business* (Washington, D.C., Govt. Print. Off., April 1975), vol. 55, no. 4, pp. 30–53.

Information on the number of students, based on the average daily attendance in public schools during the 1971–72 school year, are from the State of Virginia, Superintendent of Public Instruction, *Annual Report 1972* (Richmond, 1973); and from telephone interviews with the Prince Georges County Board of Education, Office of Student Accounting, and the Montgomery County Board of Education, Office of Student Accounting.

Statistics on the market value of taxable real property per capita are based on data from the U.S. Bureau of the Census, *Current Population Reports, Estimates of the Population of Counties, July 1, 1971 and 1972,* Series P25, No. 517 (May 1974); and *Census of Governments 1972, Taxable Property Values and Assessment–Sales Price Ratios* (Washington, D.C., Govt. Print. Off.), vol. 2, pt. 1, table 4, pp. 47 and 73; and pt. 2, table 11, pp. 76–77, and 100–101. The market value is calculated as the "1971 assessed value of locally assessed real property subject to tax" divided by the "1971 median assessment sales price ratio of all types of real property" for each jurisdiction.

The two wealthiest jurisdictions, Arlington County and Falls Church, have such high break-even lines that no households with children are profitable unless household incomes are well above $25,000. In relatively poor Prince William County, on the other hand, twelve of the eighteen types are profitable, including one-student households with incomes above $6,000 and two-student households with incomes above $15,000. The precise location of the break-even lines and the exact number of household types which would be profitable are not important, since these can easily be modified by altering a few details of the methodology, but the general tendency for wealthier communities to have higher break-even lines is significant. As a consequence, two communities with different wealth levels, both using fiscal impact studies to guide their land use decisions, could reach different conclusions regarding identical development proposals.

The Amounts of Profits and Deficits

For some purposes a local government would desire to know, not only whether a particular household would bring the government a profit or a deficit, but also the amount of that profit or deficit. Among other things, this will depend on the wealth of the jurisdiction, the costs per need unit, and the amount of revenue from nonlocal sources.

In general, of two communities having the same cost per need unit, the richer one would attribute smaller profits to profitable households and larger deficits to unprofitable ones. Of course, since the two communities would have different break-even lines, some households would be unprofitable to the richer community but profitable to the poorer one. Relatively rich Falls Church, as is shown in figure 2-2, would have gained $900 from the most profitable type of household, while relatively poor Fairfax County, which had per capita expenditures nearly equal to those of Falls Church,[11] would have gained $1,200 from the same household. On the other hand, the most unprofitable household would have caused a deficit of $1,900 in Falls Church compared with a $1,200 deficit in Fairfax County. The explanation, of course, is that at a given cost per need unit, each household in a rich community costs as much in services as it would in a poor community, but it contributes less revenue since it pays lower tax rates.

[11] U.S. Bureau of the Census, *Census of Governments, 1972*, pp. 271–273.

Generally, in two communities of equal wealth having the same break-even line, the one with a higher cost per need unit would attribute higher profits to households above, and larger deficits to those below the break-even line. Clearly, if two communities are identical except that one spends twice as much per need unit, the one spending more also has to have twice the tax rate in order to balance its budget. The difference between the local government's costs and revenues for identical households, whether positive or negative, would also be twice as much in the community with the greater expenditures per need unit.

The Washington, D.C., SMSA does not have a simple example of this effect since no two communities exist with identical wealth but with different expenditures per need unit. However, it should be noted (figure 2-2) that Montgomery County, which had the largest expenditures per capita,[12] would have attributed a $1,900 profit and a $2,200 deficit to the best and worst households, respectively. Both figures are considerably larger than the corresponding figures for other jurisdictions resembling Montgomery County in wealth. Furthermore, Loudoun County, which had the lowest expenditures per capita and per student,[13] would have gained only $700 on the most profitable household and lost only $700 on the most unprofitable; both figures are low when compared with corresponding ones for most of the other jurisdictions.

EFFECTS OF FISCAL IMPACT POLICIES

Alternative Policies Based on Fiscal Impact Studies
The effects of the widespread use of fiscal impact studies depend, of course, on which fiscal impact policies, if any, local governments follow using these studies. The term *fiscal impact policy* is used here to indicate any policy of basing land use decisions on fiscal impact studies with the objective of maintaining or increasing the local government's wealth. Although they may have similar objectives, fiscal impact policies should be distinguished from other very general land use policies which do not employ fiscal impact studies of particular developments or sub-areas within the jurisdiction. For example, a general, large-lot zoning law would not be classified as a fiscal impact policy.

[12] Ibid.
[13] Ibid.

The "no-deficit" criterion.   A local government could pursue a policy of rejecting any development proposal which, according to its fiscal impact study, would cause a deficit. Here we shall refer to it as the "no-deficit" criterion. It could be applied singly or in conjunction with other, perhaps aesthetic or environmental, criteria.[14] If successfully administered, this policy would make a local government richer.

Charging fiscal impact fees.   Alternatively, a local government could permit development on the condition that the developer or occupants pay a fiscal impact fee equal to the estimated deficit. The term *fiscal impact fee* is intended to distinguish development fees based on the conclusions of fiscal impact studies from other types. (See chapter 6 for a further discussion of taxes on new developments.) Since, in most fiscal impact studies, the size of the deficit is inversely related to the income or house value of a typical household and positively related to that household's demand for services, fiscal impact fees will vary in the same way. They increase with some indicator of demand, such as the number of children or the number of bedrooms within a household, and at a given level of demand they are strongly regressive. That is, the absolute amount of the fee increases as household income or property value decreases.[15] Since deficits may recur annually, developments would have to be charged either the present value of future deficits once and for all or charged a fiscal impact fee every year.

If some new developments are profitable and unprofitable ones pay fees, local governments charging fiscal impact fees would become

[14] I am not aware that any local government actually uses an explicit no-deficit criterion. However, recently such a proposal has been made for Prince Georges County, Maryland, but has not been adopted. See Peat, Marwick, Mitchell and Company, *Prince Georges County, Maryland, Economic Development Program* (Upper Marlboro, Prince Georges County Economic Development Commission, September 1974) p. 79.

The consultant recommended, "Before a development project proposal could undergo any other stage of the County development process, it would be analyzed according to a standardized County methodology to determine its estimated fiscal impact. . . . A favorable fiscal review would be required before a project could be submitted to any other stage of the development process."

[15] For a development fee schedule with these characteristics, see Prince William County, Virginia, Planning Office, *Net Public Cost Funds: Policies and Procedures for the Calculation, Collection and Administration* (Manassas, January 1974). The fee schedule was in effect during part of 1974. Only the capital cost of schools was included in the fee.

Loudoun County, Va., also charges a similar fee which is calculated individually for all development proposals requiring a rezoning.

wealthier. Thus, fee charging is probably as attractive a policy for a local government as a no-deficits policy. Many local governments, however, lack the legal authority to charge fiscal impact fees. The California Supreme Court approved the cash development fees imposed by local governments, but courts in Florida and Arizona have not.[16] None of these court cases, however, specifically involved fiscal impact fees.

Fiscal balancing. Fiscal impact studies could also be used to calculate the profits and deficits of development proposals, thus enabling local governments to balance the deficits of some new developments with fiscal profits from others.[17] (In interviews, several staff members of local governments indicated that this was an objective of the fiscal impact studies undertaken within their jurisdictions.) A local government which precisely offsets the deficits from some new developments with profits from others would maintain its original level of wealth. Consequently, fiscal balancing is not as advantageous as other fiscal impact policies for local governments.

Effects on New Housing

Since fiscal impact results from the combined characteristics of a structure and of its inhabitants, a perfectly effective fiscal impact policy requires total governmental control over both residential construction and household movement. Of course, local governments cannot directly exclude deficit-causing households, and some migrants will be able to defeat fiscal impact policies by occupying used housing or an unanticipated type of new housing. Lacking control of household movements, local governments can only exercise fiscal impact policies imperfectly

[16] Congressional Research Service, Library of Congress, *Toward a National Growth Policy: Federal and State Developments in 1973* (Washington, D.C., Govt. Print. Off., 1974), pp. 17–18.

[17] See Maryland–National Capital Park and Planning Commission *Proposed Staging Policy, Prince Georges County, Maryland* (Riverdale, May 1973). This is a detailed account of what is essentially a fiscal-balancing proposal: "In an effort to assure that the pace of growth recommended in this policy will improve the economic and fiscal position of the County, it is recommended that existing quantifiable relationships between . . . assessed value and population be established as thresholds. Whenever population growth is shown to be increasing at a faster rate than at-place employment and/or assessed value, . . . the recommended population growth rate should be reevaluated with an eye toward restoring the balance to the threshold level" (p. 29).

Note that since the planning commission defines assessment value per capita as a wealth indicator, the "threshold level" is the break-even line.

by selectively restricting new housing according to its financial and physical characteristics. If many local governments used these policies, they
would collectively affect the amount, types, and locations of new housing throughout a metropolitan area.

The most extreme and predictable consequences would result from
strict application of the no-deficit criterion by all local governments. A
rich jurisdiction would tend to approve those types of housing designed
to attract households with a high ratio of resource to need units. In
practice, the most likely to be approved are luxury high-rise apartments,
suitable for middle- to high-income households without school-age children, and extremely expensive single-family homes. A jurisdiction having
a medium level of wealth would be likely to accept any of the housing
proposals approved by the richer jurisdictions and, additionally, might
accept new housing units likely to be inhabited by households with
lower ratios of resource to need units, for example, small, modestly
priced apartments, medium-priced townhouses, or single-family detached
homes. The poorest local government would be likely to endorse any
proposal acceptable to the richer communities but might also approve
housing for families having relatively low resource to need unit ratios,
such as garden apartments, or possibly even mobile home parks for
families with children.[18] Some households with low ratios of need to
resource units could face a serious housing shortage throughout the
metropolitan area because all local governments, even the poorest, might
reject all proposals for suitable housing by applying the no-deficit
criterion.

In general, if local governments refused to accept any housing for
households below the community's break-even line, households with

---

[18] For selected examples of fiscal impact studies exhibiting this pattern of con-
clusions, see Ann Arbor Planning Department, *The Ann Arbor Growth Study*
(Ann Arbor, Mich., October 1972); David Boyce, Bruce Allen, and co-workers,
*Phase One Report: Impact of Rapid Transit on Suburban Residential Property
Values and Land Development* (Philadelphia, Wharton School, University of
Pennsylvania, November 1972) ch. 9; Doxiadis Urban Systems, Inc., *Fiscal and
Land Use Analysis of Prince Georges County, Final Report* (Washington, D.C.,
Doxiadis, June 1970) 3 vols.; and Louis K. Lowenstein and David W. Walters,
Municipal Cost/Revenue Analysis for PUDs (Berkeley, Institute of Urban and
Regional Development, University of California, 1973) special report no. 9.
Conclusions regarding mobile homes depend a great deal on whether they are
used primarily by retired persons or by young families. For example, see San
Luis Obispo Planning Department, *Residential Land Use Economic Study,
Expenditure–Revenue Comparison, Mobile Homes, Single Family, Multiple Family*
(San Luis Obispo, Calif., 1970)

high ratios of resource to need units would, in comparison with those having low ratios, enjoy better locations, more desirable services, lower taxes relative to the services received, and a higher probability of finding their preferred housing style. If households choose the richest of those communities to which they have effective access (for tax purposes or perhaps for social reasons), each new household would tend to choose that community whose break-even line the household was just above. The no-deficit criterion, then, would tend to produce socioeconomically stratified communities.

A realistic example from within the Washington, D.C., SMSA is provided by figure 2-3, which shows how many of the nine suburban jurisdictions would have accepted housing for each type of household, assuming that all jurisdictions applied the no-deficit criterion. No local jurisdiction would have restricted new housing designed to attract no-student households with incomes in excess of $4,000, but other households would have found that at least some of the local governments would not have approved housing for them. For instance, a family without students, having an income in the $10,000 to $15,000 range, would have been profitable to all nine jurisdictions, but would have been profitable only to four jurisdictions if it had one student and to none if it had two students. All one-student households with incomes below $6,000 and all two-student households below $15,000 would have caused deficits in all nine jurisdictions. If local governments used the no-deficit criterion, there would be an extreme shortage of new housing for low- and middle-income families in the area.

The other fiscal impact policies previously described are more flexible than the no-deficit criterion and would have a less restrictive effect on new housing. Since local governments would charge relatively small fees for households immediately below their break-even lines, these households could gain access to the community by paying the fee. For example, Prince William County would charge a fiscal impact fee of only $200 to a two-student family in the $10,000 to $15,000 income range; that family would effectively have access to the county since such a fee seems feasible for a family or a developer to pay. Arlington, on the other hand, would charge the same family a fiscal impact fee of almost $1,900 annually. If the fee were charged at the time a new housing unit is constructed, housing for moderate-income families would probably be severely curtailed in that county.

A. Original assumptions

Income per household ($ thousands)

	0	1	2
> $25	9	7	4
$15 – $25	9	5	1
$10 – $15	9	4	0
$6 – $10	9	1	0
$4 – $6	9	0	0
< $4	5	0	0

Students per household ⟶ 0 1 2

B. Assumption that the amount of "other revenue" attributable to each household is half of original amount

Income per household ($ thousands)

	0	1	2
> $25	9	6	2
$15 – $25	9	2	0
$10 – $15	9	1	0
$6 – $10	9	0	0
$4 – $6	7	0	0
< $4	5	0	0

Students per household ⟶ 0 1 2

C. Assumption that other costs per household are equal to the community average

Income per household ($ thousands)

	0	1	2
> $25	9	6	2
$15 – $25	9	4	1
$10 – $15	9	1	0
$6 – $10	7	1	0
$4 – $6	6	0	0
< $4	2	0	0

Students per household ⟶ 0 1 2

Fig. 2-3. Number of suburban jurisdictions in the Washington, D.C., SMSA that find development profitable under alternate assumptions.

Even if a rich jurisdiction sincerely intends to encourage modestly priced housing through fiscal balancing, it would probably approve very little of it. Again, figure 2-2 provides a realistic example of this. Relatively rich Arlington County would need the profits from ten no-student households in the $10,000 to $15,000 bracket in order to balance the deficits of one two-student household within the same income bracket. On the other hand, in Prince William County the profits from a single no-student household in the $10,000 to $15,000 bracket would cover the deficits of more than three two-student households within that same bracket. Consequently, if all local governments used a fiscal balancing policy to increase the supply of low-income housing, the outcome would be quite similar to that resulting from the use of the no-deficit criterion; households with low incomes would be concentrated in the relatively poor jurisdictions. One major difference exists between the two policies, however; under a fiscal balancing criterion some new housing for households with low incomes could be approved in the metropolitan area, whereas none might be approved under the no-deficit criterion.

In many cases the local governing body does not have the opportunity to decide which fiscal deficit is to be subsidized by which profitable development because the developer decides this before he presents his proposal. In any community using fiscal impact studies the developer has an incentive to combine profitable and unprofitable development into a single package in order to avoid the onus of presenting a deficit-causing proposal. Luxury apartments or office buildings, for example, could be used to fiscally balance town houses designed for young families.[19] If, as many people believe, developers making the fiscal balancing decisions are wary of mixing economic classes within the same development, the fiscal deficits of households with children would be balanced by the profits attributable to childless households within the same income bracket.

Effects on Existing Residents
The intended beneficiaries of any jurisdiction's fiscal impact policies are, of course, its existing residents. Critics have argued, however, that local

---

[19] This may be a necessary strategy for a developer to gain approval of residential development. For example, in the study cited in note 14, the only residential developments recommended for approval were ones which had been combined with major nonresidential developments in the developers' proposals.

governments which follow restrictive fiscal impact policies are actually doing a disservice to their residents. One argument is that it is self-defeating for a local government to use a fiscal impact policy because neighboring local governments will retaliate.[20] An attempt by a community to gain a profitable manufacturing plant while rejecting housing for the new workers, for example, would allegedly provoke neighboring communities to reject housing for the workers also. Consequently, the plant could not be located in this area.

Actually, even a blatant no-deficit policy would not necessarily provoke reprisals from neighboring jurisdictions because they would not necessarily perceive that the policy harmed them. Using the example of the Washington, D.C., SMSA, if the city of Falls Church, Virginia, accepted an office development but did not permit residential development for new office workers with children (who would be unprofitable to Falls Church), adjoining Fairfax County would be willing to permit such housing because, according to that county's fiscal impact study, such households would be profitable. Similarly, Fairfax County could accept an industrial plant, while neighboring Prince William County would willingly approve housing for many of the new workers. Provided that local jurisdictions have disparate break-even lines and follow independent fiscal impact policies, they would make complementary, rather than retaliatory, land use decisions.

However, if all jurisdictions have similar break-even lines, the effective restrictions on labor force migration into and within the metropolitan area could make it impossible to establish new industries or to expand existing ones throughout the entire area. Consequently, none of the local governments would gain the increased fiscal profit usually attributed to nonresidential development, and existing residents would lose the increased income from better employment opportunities in the area.

In some cases, fiscal balancing could provide a solution to this problem if the potential employer and a developer presented the profitable industrial facility and an unprofitable housing development as a single proposal. This approach would be in the interest of both the developer

[20] For example, see Julius Margolis, "On Municipal Land Policy for Fiscal Gains," in W. Beaton, ed., *Municipal Needs, Services and Financing: Reading on Municipal Expenditures* (New Brunswick, N.J., Center for Urban Policy Research, 1974) pp. 281–295.

and the employer, and the Planned Unit Development (PUD) concept—through which residential and commercial–industrial developments are often combined into single proposals—provides an established and practical device for creating such a combined proposal.[21] This strategy would be most successful in relatively poor jurisdictions because of their tendency to attribute large profits to developments above the break-even line and small deficits to those below the line.

Rising aspirations on the part of poor jurisdictions could also have destructive consequences. When all local governments independently pursue fiscal impact policies, migratory households tend to be concentrated between the break-even lines of their new jurisdiction and the next wealthier one. Consequently, although the absolute wealth of the jurisdictions may increase, they will tend to maintain their original rankings relative to each other. An attempt by a dissatisfied local government to increase its wealth relative to other local governments by permitting only very profitable developments would harm the wealthier governments relying on poorer governments to approve workers' housing. Because of the increased difficulty of establishing commercial–industrial development in the metropolitan area, existing residents of the wealthier communities would suffer higher taxes or poorer services than otherwise, or both, as well as loss of potential income. Such a policy would also injure those migratory households with relatively low ratios of resource to need units, which rely on poorer local governments to approve suitable housing for them. Moreover, such a policy would be detrimental to the poorer local government, for any household or industry which would be extremely profitable to it would often be profitable, although less so, to a richer jurisdiction. Given a choice, the households or industry would generally choose to locate in the richer jurisdiction because of its lower relative tax rate. Consequently, by attempting to become wealthier quickly, the local government may not become wealthier.

[21] For examples of studies of developments combining residential and industrial or commercial land uses, see New America Development Corporation, *Fiscal Impact of Cameron on the City of Alexandria, Virginia* (Alexandria, Va., New American Development Corporation, December 1973); Wainwright and Ramsey, Inc., "Study of Anticipated Economic Impact Upon the City of Alameda and the Alameda Unified School District Occasioned the Proposed Harbor Bay Isles Development on Bay Farm Island," in William T. Leonard, ed., *Growth Cost–Revenue Studies* (Berkeley, Calif., Associated Homebuilders of the Greater East Bay, Inc., 1972).

Although they are seldom considered in fiscal impact studies, property values and rents are a matter of great concern to existing residents. They would certainly be affected by fiscal impact policies through the effects of such policies on new housing construction. The types of housing likely to cause deficits in every jurisdiction, such as modestly priced single-family homes, garden apartments, or mobile homes suitable for families with children, would be restricted severely throughout the metropolitan area. Consequently, the value of existing units of these types could reasonably be expected to increase, which would be beneficial to existing owners but not to existing renters. Since the supply of new housing which causes profits in some communities and deficits in others would vary considerably throughout a metropolitan area, the consequences for owners and renters of existing properties of these types would be very complex, probably varying by jurisdiction.

Despite the risks that existing residents may be harmed in ways not usually considered in fiscal impact studies,[22] the proliferation of these studies suggests that existing residents concur in their use. The explanation for this may be that the immediate and readily apparent consequences of fiscal impact policies have strong support in many communities. First, such policies generally limit residential development and population growth, especially in rich communities. Growth limitations of all types seem to receive considerable local support in most areas. Second, a no-deficit criterion assures existing residents that occupants of new dwellings will have property values at least as high as, and in most cases higher than, those of the existing households of similar size.[23]

[22] The need to consider changes in incomes, property values, service quality, environmental factors, etc., is often mentioned, but only a few authors attempt to quantify these changes. Attempts to quantify in dollars changes in the quality of education are discussed in the following: Stephen Levy and Robert K. Arnold, *An Evaluation of Four Growth Alternatives in the City of Milpitas, 1972–1977* (Palo Alto, Calif., Institute of Regional and Urban Studies, August 1972); Boyce et al. *Phase One Report.* One handbook for local officials includes a formula for estimating the effect of multiple-family residential construction on values of existing single-family homes: Connecticut Development Group, Inc., *Cost–Revenue Impact Analysis for Residential Developments.* For one attempt to combine fiscal environmental and social effects in assessing the overall impact of development, see Livingston and Blayney, Inc., *Open Space vs. Development: Foothills Environmental Design Study* (Palo Alto, Calif., City of Palo Alto, February 1971).

[23] In communities with some commercial or industrial property, the ratio of total assessed value to students is greater than the average assessed value per student of residential property alone. In order for the local government to break

While new households would be more heterogeneous under fee-charging or fiscal balancing policies, such policies nevertheless preclude a large influx of very poor households.

The obvious reason for local residents to support fiscal impact policies, of course, is that if deficit-causing households are admitted to the community, the existing residents either will have to pay higher taxes or receive poorer-quality services. While existing residents occasionally can avoid the effect of a deficit through a selective tax increase or quality decrease to a specific group, a deficit would normally be financed by a general tax increase to be shared by existing residents, new residents, and some nonresidents. Thus, existing households would not usually pay the entire amount, but they are probably correct in believing that a deficit-causing development would adversely affect their taxes or services, however minutely.

In general, the most immediate and conspicuous consequences of the pursuit of fiscal impact policies would probably be favorable to the existing households. Although there are pitfalls for existing residents in fiscal impact policies, these would probably be complex, delayed, and not easily detectable. Local governments with the power to pursue fiscal impact policies have a strong incentive to do so.

INTERGOVERNMENTAL TRANSFERS

While most intergovernmental transfers are not intended to affect land use decisions, transfers do provide a possible mechanism through which state governments could change the fiscal incentives of local governments using fiscal impact policies to modify the consequences of such policies previously described.[24] Even if it wanted to do so, a state government could not avoid influencing the outcome of local governments' fiscal impact policies. Intergovernmental transfers from the state government appear as revenue in local governments' fiscal impact studies, affecting their conclusions.

---

even, each new householder must have a higher assessed value than an identical existing household. This also implies that most existing residents cause "deficits," which are subsidized by "profitable" commercial and industrial properties.

[24] Most of the comments regarding state governments could also apply to the federal government.

Transfers Decreasing the Costs of Local Governments

In a commonly used transfer scheme, the state government disburses money to local governments at a flat rate per need unit; a state, for example, might distribute statewide aid to education at a hundred dollars per student. Assuming that local governments do not increase their expenditures by the full amount of the transfer, the transfer reduces the locally financed cost per need unit and reduces local taxes. On a fiscal impact study a reduced cost per need unit would cause decreased profits and deficits. In fee-charging jurisdictions, intergovernmental transfers of this type would benefit migratory households by reducing the amount of the fiscal impact fees they would be required to pay in certain jurisdictions. The effect of intergovernmental transfers on the decisions of local governments which use fiscal balancing is uncertain. Since changes in expenditures per need unit have no effect on the wealth or break-even line of a local government, flat-rate transfers would have no effect on the land use decisions of local governments using a strict no-deficit criterion. This would not necessarily be the case, however, if the transfers were a function of the need units of new households, rather than all households. For example, if a state government paid local governments one hundred dollars per student for new students only, the break-even line for the whole community would be unaffected, but that for new households would be shifted downward.

Transfers Changing the Wealth of Local Government

Some intergovernmental transfers are equivalent to revenue from additional resource units and, therefore, make the local government wealthier. Examples of this include payments in lieu of taxes, Forest Service royalties to local governments from timber harvests, or, in general, any grant or payment which is not closely related to the number of need units in the community. Since wealthier jurisdictions have higher break-even lines and are more restrictive of new development than are poorer ones, these types of intergovernmental transfers worsen the consequences of fiscal impact policies for households desiring to move.

That state governments assume most or all of the financial responsibility for education and other major social services has been suggested as a means of reducing the fiscal incentives of local governments to exclude certain types of households.[25] In the case of education, this

---

[25] For example, see Charles M. Harr, ed., *The President's Task Force on Suburban Problems, Final Report* (Cambridge, Mass., Ballinger, 1968) p. 70.

could be done either through state payments which cover all of the educational costs of local governments or by direct state administration of the educational system. Each jurisdiction would have to redefine its wealth and its break-even line, substituting some need unit such as persons for school children, since the number of children would no longer be an appropriate indicator of demand for local government services. So long as a local government finances any services from general local taxes, it has a break-even line which could be either raised or lowered when the jurisdiction revises its wealth indicator. Consequently, financing education at the state level would not necessarily benefit those households seeking new housing should local governments continue to use fiscal impact policies. Those jurisdictions which become richer as a result of the redefinition of wealth would be more restrictive of new residential development, and others, less so. It would, however, substantially reduce the deficits of households with children, and local governments would have less incentive to restrict family housing.

The proposal to remove industrial and commercial property as a local government resource, subjecting it instead to uniform taxation by the state government, has been suggested as a way to comply with state court decisions to the effect that wide differences among school districts in expenditures per pupil, caused by the present tax structure, are unconstitutional.[26] Except for those few jurisdictions without commercial or industrial property, the removal of such property from the tax bases of local governments would make them poorer, often substantially so. As a result, in most jurisdictions more households would be profitable, and of the jurisdictions. From the viewpoint of the migratory households, smaller deficits would be attributed to those below the break-even lines this proposal would have excellent consequences, since most jurisdictions, including those which practice a no-deficit policy, would be willing to approve a broader range of housing; fees in fee-charging jurisdictions would decrease; and fiscal balancing would be facilitated.

Redistributive Transfers
In contrast to flat-rate transfers, which depend only upon need units within a community, redistributive transfers—intended to cover a higher proportion of the costs of relatively poor local governments than of

[26] Robert W. Hartman and Robert D. Reischauer, *The Effects of Reform in School Finance on the Level and Distribution of Tax Burdens* (Washington, D.C., Brookings Institution, 1974) p. 145.

relatively rich ones—generally are positively related to need units but negatively related to resource units. Consequently, in assessing any fiscal impact of new households, local governments would attribute a larger increase in intergovernmental revenues to low-income households than to high-income ones. For example, in 1972 the state of Virginia distributed most of its educational funds by a formula which deducted 0.6 percent of real property value in the local jurisdiction from the amount which the state would otherwise pay based on a complicated formula which included the number of students.[27] Development which increased real property values without proportionately increasing the number of students would therefore have decreased total state transfers to the jurisdiction. This particular formula was weakly redistributive; transfers attributable to the households with less than $4,000 income were approximately $200 more than transfers for households having more than $25,000 income with the same number of school children.

In a program with similar consequences, the state simply pays local governments for certain residents likely to cause deficits. For example, the 1968 President's Task Force on Suburban Problems recommended that the federal government pay local governments $200 for every elementary school-aged child of a Vietnam war veteran.[28] The apparent purpose of this recommendation was to increase the amount of transfer revenues which local governments would attribute to low- or moderate-income households with children, a group which causes deficits in many jurisdictions, and to reduce the fiscal incentives of local governments to exclude these households.

While any transfer program which, in effect, pays local governments to accept households with low ratios of resource to need units increases the probability that the low-ratio households will break even, both of these particular examples would have little effect on rich jurisdictions because of the small sums involved. As can be seen from figure 2-2, a payment of $200 per student for new families with incomes of $10,000 or less would not have made any such household profitable to the five wealthiest of the suburban jurisdictions in the Washington, D.C., SMSA in 1972, although such payments would, of course, have decreased the deficit attributable to these households. In Arlington, the wealthiest of

[27] Virginia Education Association, *ABC's of School Finance* (Richmond, Va., June 1972).
[28] Harr, *The President's Task Force,* pp. 151–153.

these jurisdictions, over $1,000 per child would have been necessary to make one- and two-student families in the $6,000 to $10,000 bracket break even. Small payments of $200 per student would have caused a few categories of medium- and low-income households to become profitable in the four poorest jurisdictions, however, while payments of $1,000 per student would have been a windfall to the relatively poor jurisdictions.

Small transfer payments could effectively increase the supply of deficit-producing housing, but most of the increase would be in relatively poor jurisdictions. There would not be a tendency for relatively rich communities to become more heterogeneous, although this tendency would increase with the size of the grant. A program to neutralize all fiscal incentives to exclude certain housing without making existing residents better off would require payments equal to each migratory household's anticipated fiscal deficit; the state government under such a transfer program would make large payments to rich jurisdictions and small ones to poor jurisdictions for the identical households. Such a program would be redistributive to migratory households who would gain access to more desirable communities with better services or lower taxes, rather than to the local governments or their existing residents who would be unaffected.

CONCLUSIONS

Implicit in the fiscal impact literature is the belief that it is reasonable for local governments to expect households to "pay their own way." Actually, this is not reasonable because it is not possible. First, if the local government finances its services from general taxes, it is mathematically impossible for every type of land use to break even or to produce a profit. If any land use produces a profit, the tax rate is lowered to balance the budget, so that another land use causes a deficit. As a practical matter, most households cause deficits to their local governments because the governments generally derive a profit from the nonresidential land uses in their jurisdictions.

Second, a system under which all taxpayers must help to pay for a service regardless of the use they make of it is redistributive from nonusers to users of this service. Education and many other services have traditionally been financed this way, on the rationale that society gains important external benefits from their provision. Fiscal deficits of house-holds, as they are usually computed, are largely composed of costs for services, primarily education, which are necessarily and purposefully redistributive to users. A fiscal impact fee is therefore essentially a charge to the recipient of a redistributive service for the cost of the service deliberately provided for him by the local government.

By putting a fiscal impact policy into effect, a local government rejects the traditional rationale and method for providing certain types of services. But it has good reasons for doing so. The costs of certain public services are concentrated within a small area, but the external benefits are diffused. The existing residents of any jurisdiction gain basically the same external benefits from living in a literate society, but at much less cost to themselves, when some other jurisdiction provides the education. Existing residents understandably tend to resist increments in costs without increments in benefits.

Despite the fact that fiscal impact policies are a rejection of the traditional method of providing some public services and that such policies have adverse consequences for some people, state governments may tolerate limited use of fiscal impact policies for pragmatic reasons. A local government with significant power to regulate land use probably has the means to utilize fiscal impact policies, but the state government would have difficulty policing the thoughts of local decision makers. To preclude the regulation of land use for fiscal purposes, the state government may have to limit the power of localities to regulate land use for any purpose, or take over the decision-making power itself. Some state governments may be reluctant to take such strong and controversial actions. First, it would be politically difficult to do so, since the existing constituents of elected local officials are, to a considerable extent, also the existing constituents of elected state officials. Second, if the state forbids the use of all fiscal criteria, it must either deregulate all land use or devise an alternative criterion for land use decisions, which is practical, politically acceptable, has desirable results, and precludes the use of fiscal impact policies. Devising such a criterion would be a difficult task. Third, the state government may prefer that local governments give some consideration to the fiscal consequences of their land use decisions, fearing that, if they do not, the state governments will have to rescue some local governments from their fiscal problems.

If the state government accepts the use of some fiscal impact criteria by local governments, a moderate fiscal impact policy would probably be preferable to traditional fiscal zoning policies. Existing residents would prefer the former because it should more effectively prevent them from paying any part of the costs of development. Fiscal zoning, such as large-lot zoning or minimum building size requirements, is based on the assumption that large, expensive single-family homes are generally profitable, which may not be correct. Households seeking apartments would generally prefer the effects of fiscal impact policies, since some apartments (often entirely excluded by fiscal zoning), are profitable and would be permitted by some local governments. Because fiscal impact policies at least create the possibility of varied types of new residential construction in different jurisdictions, migratory households would generally be better off under fiscal impact policies than under fiscal zoning, although in both cases many may be effectively excluded from some jurisdictions. However, households desiring high-cost, single-family detached housing—usually the type favored by local officials under traditional fiscal zoning—may be worse off under fiscal impact policies, since this type of housing might be restricted or charged fees in some communities.

By establishing some limitations on the use of fiscal impact policies and by using intergovernmental transfers purposefully to influence the decisions of local governments, the state government could mitigate the consequences of fiscal impact policies for migratory households, while leaving existing households no worse off fiscally. Consequently, existing households and their local governments would have no fiscal incentives to oppose such limitations. In the paragraphs that follow, I will discuss some possible criteria.

First, the state government could forbid local governments to use the no-deficit criterion. The effects of this criterion on migratory households are more severe than the effects of other fiscal impact policies. Also, the state government has limited ability to influence, via intergovernmental transfers, the decisions of local governments using the no-deficit criteria. However, the state government may want to exclude the poorest local governments from this prohibition in order that they may become wealthier.

Second, the state could insist that local governments apply a fiscal balancing policy and that they approve widely varying types of deficit-producing development. This would increase the availability of housing to those who would suffer severe shortages under a no-deficit criterion, broaden the socioeconomic range of new residents in all communities, and leave the existing residents no worse off. Two risks are inherent in this recommendation, however. Initially, since the local governments would not receive a net fiscal gain from approving such developments, they might cease approving developments entirely. The state government which desired to mitigate the inequities to migratory households would have to prevent that reaction, perhaps by allowing local governments to retain some fiscal profit or by requiring that all local governments approve some development. The other risk falls upon the existing residents. Given the state of the art of fiscal impact studies, they could not hope to balance profits and deficits precisely, and careless methodology could leave them worse off.

Third, the state government could allow local governments to charge fiscal impact fees, and the state government should be prepared to intervene directly to increase some types of housing by paying the fees. Compulsory fees may have to be enforced, as local governments may have nonfiscal reasons to oppose some residential development. While it may be controversial, local jurisdictions may regard this method of intervention more positively than they would an overruling of local zoning laws by judicial or legislative action.

Fourth, the state should see that none of its intergovernmental transfer programs create incentives for local governments to act in opposition to the state's land use policies. The state government may want to use intergovernmental transfers deliberately to facilitate fiscal balancing by making payments for those households which often cause deficits.

Finally, the state government should help to improve the methodology of fiscal impact studies and make it available to local jurisdictions. One of the incentives to use the no-deficit criterion is that a local government can conclude that a development produces a profit with considerably more confidence that it can determine the amount of that profit. If the state government insists that the local governments take fees or engage in fiscal balancing, it should help them to reduce the risks of making serious errors.

APPENDIX A

The following is an explanation of the methods and assumptions used in the fiscal impact study sample based on the Washington, D.C., SMSA.

Revenues

Real property taxes. The estimates are weighted, total effective tax rates based on the actual, rather than nominal, assessment rates.

Income taxes. Montgomery and Prince Georges counties, Maryland, collect income taxes from residents. Effective tax rate estimates for money income brackets, based on data from Greene, Neenan, and Scott,[29] were applied to the midpoint of the ranges in order to estimate the county's revenue from households in each income bracket.

Sales taxes. Local jurisdictions in Virginia retain one-fourth of the state-collected sales tax revenues. Estimates from Greene et al. of the effective tax rate paid to Virginia jurisdictions by Virginians were used. Their finding that the tax was slightly regressive biases the fiscal impact study slightly in favor of low-income developments. It was assumed that sales taxes were paid to the residents' own jurisdictions, an assumption that favors development in jurisdictions lacking strong retail concentrations. In general, the amount of the estimated sales tax revenues was small, and minor differences in assumptions would have had little effect on the profits and deficits projected by the fiscal impact studies.

Personal property taxes. No personal property tax revenue was attributed to residential development in Maryland counties, since it is a business tax. Virginia jurisdictions tax vehicles, using differing assessment and tax rates. Based on estimates by Greene et al. of vehicle tax revenue as a proportion of a personal property tax,[30] and the 1970 census data on the number of automobiles in the jurisdictions,[31] it appears that most collected from twenty-five to thirty-five dollars per automobile in 1970. A thirty-dollar personal property tax revenue per vehicle was used for all jurisdictions and distributed among income groups by 1970 census data on the "number of automobiles available." Because high-income households have more automobiles, this distribution is favorable to them.

[29] Kenneth Greene, William Neenan, and Claudia Scott, *Fiscal Interactions in a Metropolitan Area* (Lexington, Mass., D. C. Heath, 1974).
[30] Ibid.
[31] Maryland Comptroller of the Treasury, *Summary Report.*

Other revenues from local sources.   "Other" revenues, a substantial amount of money in all jurisdictions, come from myriad sources, some paid directly by households and some by businesses. Greene et al. found that most of the minor local and state taxes in the Washington, D.C., area were regressive, with the lowest-income bracket paying rates two or three times those paid by the highest-income bracket.[32] It was assumed arbitrarily that "other" taxes and fees were regressive with the lowest group paying three times the rate of the highest group. For each jurisdiction, the assumed rates would have produced the actual 1972 tax revenue, based on aggregate money income for each income bracket in 1969, as reported in the 1970 census. Comparable 1972 income data, if available, would have been much larger, and, consequently, the assumed 1972 tax rates and the revenue attributed to all income groups were overstated. Figure A-1 shows that if other revenue were arbitrarily assumed to be half the amount originally assumed for all income brackets, keeping the assumption of regressiveness, the break-even lines of most jurisdictions would shift upward significantly.

Intergovernmental transfers from the federal government.   These were allocated on a simple per household basis, a pro-development assumption since most federal revenues were for impacted school districts and education-related programs, which would not necessarily increase proportionately with the number of households.

Intergovernmental transfers from the state.   The response of the state's transfer program to changes in local population were included to the extent possible, rather than using the typical assumption that transfers will continue at the same rate (per student, per household, per capita, or per dollar of local expenditure).

Transfers for *highways* are distributed to cities on a road mileage basis in Virginia. Except for Arlington, counties are not responsible for roads and do not receive highway funds. It was assumed that there was no relationship between population and road mileage in these jurisdictions (since they are all relatively well developed) and that no increase in state transfers for highways results from increased population.

Maryland distributes highway funds from earmarked sources to counties based on road mileage and population. It was assumed, based on

---

[32] Greene et al., *Fiscal Interactions.*

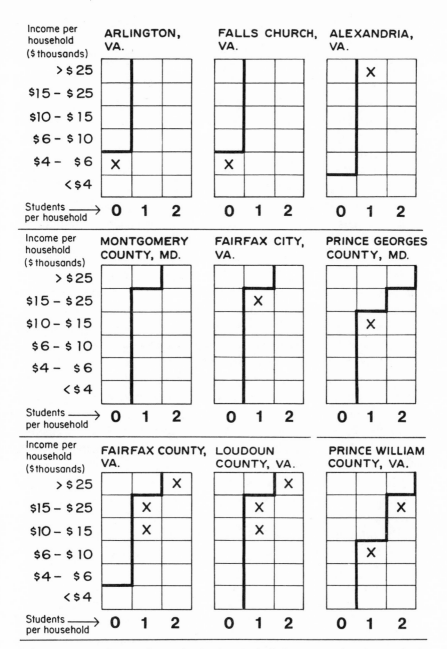

Fig. A-1. Break-even lines of suburban jurisdictions assuming that "other" revenues attributable to each household were equal to half of the amount originally assumed. X indicates the group which was profitable under original assumptions but is not profitable under the above assumption.

41

information supplied by the Maryland Department of Transportation, that transfers for highways amounted to roughly twenty dollars per person. No change in lane mileage was assumed to occur.

Concerning *welfare,* the Virginia Department of Social Welfare indicated that the rule of thumb in 1972 was that the state reimbursed counties for 80 percent of welfare expenditures, the figure used here.

Maryland also reimbursed 80 percent of county expenditures for selected welfare programs, but for others the county was required to contribute a specified number of cents on its tax rate. As the cumulative effect of these systems was unclear, it was assumed arbitrarily that the state transfers covered the same proportion of additional welfare expenditures as of its total welfare expenditures in 1972.

Regarding *education,* most transfers for educational operating expenses in Virginia were distributed by a formula which included the true market value of real estate, the number of elementary and high school students, and the qualifications of the teachers employed. Jurisdictions received larger increments in transfers from low-cost developments than from high-cost developments and would have had decreased transfers as a result of developments with no students. This transfer formula mildly favored low-cost developments over high-cost developments (assuming each had the same number of students), and it was mildly unfavorable to households without students. Sales taxes earmarked for education were distributed at the rate of $72 per student in 1972. Small amounts of revenue from other educational programs in the Virginia jurisdictions were allocated on a per student basis.

Montgomery and Prince Georges counties received almost the "per student" minimum payment specified in Maryland's basic educational transfer formula.

The *other transfers* not included in the highway, welfare, and educational categories were allocated on a per household basis.

Expenditures

Education. For each jurisdiction, it was assumed that the marginal operating costs of additional students equaled total education expenditures divided by the average daily public school attendance. The average ranged from $830 to over $1,500 and was the most important determinant of whether households with school children were profitable or unprofitable. Since some expenditures were for administration and services other than the regular public schools, the total average expenditure per student may be an overestimate of the marginal costs. Assuming instead that marginal costs per student were only three-quarters of the average would have shifted the break-even line down in most jurisdictions.

Welfare. Since local jurisdictions could not provide appropriate data, it was assumed that the total 1972 welfare expenditures in each jurisdiction were distributed among income groups according to Bureau of the Census data.[33] Estimated welfare expenditures as a percentage of estimated total 1969 income for each income bracket was calculated, and this percentage was applied to the midpoint of each income range in order to estimate the average welfare expenditure per household in each income bracket. The average is overstated, as are all figures which depend on income distributions from the 1970 census. Welfare payments are a function of the number of children, since Aid to Families with Dependent Children is the largest program. Because of lack of data, however, payments were allocated on a per household basis, resulting in an unfavorable assumption for low-income, childless households but a favorable assumption for those with children.

Other expenditures. It was arbitrarily assumed that other expenditures per household were equal to one-half of the community average per household in 1972. This figure was used on the theory that many expenditures are not for services to households and therefore would not rise proportionately with households. This is a common assumption in fiscal impact studies. Frequently, the proportion of expenditures attributable to resident households is assumed to be the same as their proportion of total assessed value, an assumption which could not be used here due to lack of data.

As shown in figure A-2, the assumption that marginal "other" costs are equal to the average per household (a strongly antidevelopment assumption) shifts the break-even line upward in most communities.

[33] U.S. Bureau of the Census. "Money Income in 1973 of Families and Persons in the United States," in *Current Population Reports.* Series P60, no. 97 (Washington, D.C., Govt. Print. Off., 1975), table 6.

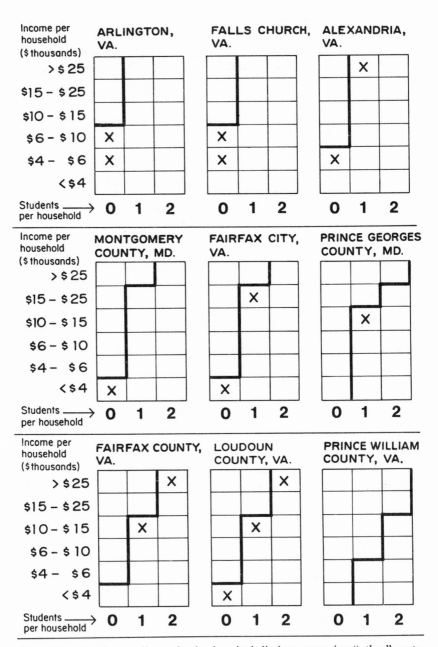

Fig. A-2. Break-even lines of suburban jurisdictions assuming "other" costs per household equal to community average. X indicates household which was profitable under original assumptions but is not profitable under the above assumption.

44

Data Sources

The basic sources for expenditures and revenue data for jurisdictions in the Washington, D.C., SMSA are two reports from the U.S. Bureau of the Census: *Census of Governments, 1972. Local Government in Metropolitan Areas,* vol. 5; and *Local Government Finances in Selected Metropolitan Areas and Large Counties: 1971–72,* series GF72, no. 6.

Capital outlays, interest and debt service, and all revenues and expenditures for utilities (except sewerage) have been excluded. The data are totals for all governments within the specified geographic area, including municipalities, independent agencies, and county governments. Supplementary data were obtained from the publications which follow.

Assessment ratios. The effective tax rates were estimated by multiplying assessment ratios by weighted total nominal tax rates, as reported in state publications.

U.S. Bureau of the Census, *Census of Governments, 1972. Taxable Property Values and Assessment—Sales Price Ratios: Assessment—Sales Price Ratios and Tax Rates* (Washington, D.C., Govt. Print. Off., 1973) vol. 2, pt. 2, table 11.

Tax rates. The tax rates are totals for all governments within the geographic area, weighted by the 1970 populations of the areas affected by each tax rate.

Maryland Department of Fiscal Services, Division of Fiscal Research, *Local Government Finances in Maryland for the Fiscal Year Ended June 30, 1972* (Annapolis, Maryland Department of Fiscal Services, 1973).

Virginia Municipal League, *Tax Rates in Virginia Cities and Urban Counties, 1972* (Richmond, Virginia Municipal League, p. 3).

Transfers from state governments. Data on state transfers to local governments were compiled from state reports.

Maryland Department of Education, *106th Annual Report* (Baltimore, Maryland Department of Education, 1975) tables 121 and 124.

Virginia Auditor of Public Accounts, *Report of the Auditor of Public Accounts of Commonwealth of Virginia on Comparative Cost of City Government, Year Ended June 30, 1972* and *Report on Comparative*

Cost of County Government, Year Ended June 30, 1972 (Richmond, Virginia Auditor of Public Accounts, 1974).

Maryland Department of Transportation, *1972 Annual Report* (Baltimore, Maryland Department of Transportation, 1974).

Maryland Department of Social Services, *1972 Annual Report* (Baltimore, Maryland Department of Social Services, 1974).

Data on characteristics of the population in the various jurisdictions were obtained from the 1970 census, and other U.S. Bureau of the Census publications.

For income distribution in Virginia, see the U.S. Bureau of the Census, *General Social and Economic Characteristics Final Report* PC(1)–C48, Virginia (Washington, D.C., Govt. Print. Off., 1973).

For 1970 population of county subdivisions in Maryland and Virginia, see the U.S. Bureau of the Census, *U.S. Census of Population, 1970, Number of Inhabitants. Final Report* PC(1)–A22, Maryland and *Final Report* PC(1)–A48, Virginia (Washington, D.C., Govt. Print. Off., 1971).

For automobiles by income class in the Washington, D.C., SMSA, see the U.S. Bureau of the Census, *Census of Housing: 1970, Metropolitan Housing Characteristics. Final Report* HC(2)–232 (Washington, D.C., Govt. Print. Off., 1972).

For population of households, and their number and size in Maryland and Virginia, see the U.S. Bureau of the Census, *Census of Population 1970, Characteristics of the Population,* vol. 1, pts. 22–48 (Washington, D.C., Govt. Print. Off., 1971).

The number of households in 1972 were estimated, assuming the same household size as that in 1970 and the same number of persons in group quarters.

U.S. Department of the Census, *Current Population Reports, Population Estimates and Projections, Estimates of the Population of Counties. July 1, 1971 and 1972.* Series P25, No. 515 (May 1974).

The housing values were based on the 1971 median value of one-unit, owner-occupied, mortgaged properties acquired during 1967 through early 1971, as classified by 1970 U.S. income brackets.

U.S. Department of the Census, *Census of Housing 1970. Residential Finance,* vol. V, table 16, p. 127 (March 1973).

The housing values by income range used in the fiscal impact studies were as follows:

Income range	Housing value
Less than $4,000	$11,500
$4,000–$6,000	$14,200
$6,000–$10,000	$16,400
$10,000–$15,000	$22,300
$15,000–$25,000	$30,000
$25,000 and over	$47,900

3 / JON C. SONSTELIE AND PAUL R. PORTNEY

Property Value Maximization as a Decision Criterion for Local Governments

COMMUNITIES AND PRIVATE FIRMS are similar in that both produce goods and services for the direct or indirect satisfaction of consumer wants. For communities, these goods and services include elementary and high school education, garbage collection, police protection, recreation, and road maintenance. Many of these services are also provided by private firms which, of course, provide many other kinds of goods and services as well. In fact, most services provided by local governments are not "public goods," according to the economist's definition of a public good, but are merely publicly provided private goods. On purely technological grounds, most of these local public services could be and are privately provided.

While there appears to be little difference between the basic function of communities and firms as producers of goods and services, or even between the types of goods and services they produce, they certainly differ with respect to the way in which they make those goods and services available to consumers. The services produced by private firms are offered for sale at a specified price, and consumers can choose freely the amount of each that they wish to purchase. For publicly provided services, however, residents must consume the amount provided by their community, and they pay for these services through a tax assessment,

The authors are affiliated with Resources for the Future.

which is unrelated to most of their service demands. Through the political process, residents may influence the quantity or quality of the services they receive, but they cannot choose, as they can with goods provided by private firms, how much they will consume independently of the choices of other consumers.

Because its goods or services are sold in a market, a private firm has a clear-cut measure of performance to guide its production and distribution decisions. This measure is the dollar profit of the firm—the difference between the amount consumers pay for its output and the cost of producing that output.[1] However, the community has no comparable measure of performance to guide it in its production of public services. It is true, of course, that the citizens of a community can and do register their opinions about the quality of the public services being provided and the amount they are paying to finance those services. Citizens express these opinions through their votes on education or general tax rate referenda, by support for particular candidates for the school board and city council, and by direct participation in public meetings of local boards and councils. However, these expressions of public opinion cannot easily be translated into simple terms of revenue and cost as they can in the case of private firms.

One criterion for public decision making, which has gained some popularity at the federal level and is now being used increasingly at the state and local levels, is cost–benefit analysis. On a project-by-project basis, cost–benefit analysis does attempt to convert into money terms those factors relevant to the undertaking of a public project. However, it is by its very nature a partial approach. Projects are considered singly, or with others, in a piecemeal fashion with no overall goal in mind. While policy makers know that they are to efficiently allocate resources to specific public services, they are not aware of the goal toward which the provision of the sum total of such services is to be directed. Under

---

[1] It is true that other objectives have been imputed to the firm, most notably, sales maximization, growth maximization, and target rate of return. However, in a recent assessment of competing theories of the firm, R. Cyert and C. Hedrick ["Theory of the Firm, Past, Present, and Future: An Interpretation," *Journal of Economic Literature* vol. 10 (1972) pp. 398–412] were forced to conclude, ". . . that there is a growing uneasiness with the neoclassical [profit maximization] approach . . . but that the above rationale is still widely held by most economists. . . . We see no evidence at this time for a substantial change despite the progress being made by current approaches."

such a system, no sweeping changes in budgetary policy, however desirable, are likely to occur. Thus, although cost–benefit analysis does evaluate in money terms the factors relevant to expenditures on public services, it is not analogous to profit maximization in the private sector because it is not an overall objective.

Some further thought suggests that such an analogue may exist, however. Within a given metropolitan area there are generally a large number of communities producing a wide variety of public services. As noted by Tiebout,[2] these alternatives offer each household some choice with respect to the quality of public services it can consume. By locating in a community whose public services suit its tastes and income, the household makes a decision not unlike those affecting its consumption of private goods.

To consume the public services of a particular community, a household must first occupy a dwelling there. The consumption benefits of a house include both its physical features and the public services of the community in which it is located. While the former classification includes the number of rooms in the house, the size of the lot, the distance to the center of the metropolitan area, etc., the latter includes the typical public services mentioned above. The physical characteristics of a house, then, are tied together with the public services of its community, and both are sold as one package.

A household occupies a dwelling either by renting or owning it. Although renting is not necessarily the most common kind of occupancy, for our purposes we will assume that everyone is a renter rather than an owner. This assumption will simplify our argument, but it will not affect our conclusions. As will be seen later, a homeowner may also be regarded as a renter who pays an imputed rent to himself.

Just as the quality of its physical characteristics affects the rent charged for a house so, too, will the quality of the public services in the community in which it is located. For example, with everything else being equal, communities with better than average schools will have above average housing rents. The positive impact of public service quality on rent has, in fact, been verified by Orr.[3] A similar relationship between public service quality and the selling prices of homes has been

[2] C. Tiebout, "A Pure Theory of Local Expenditures," *Journal of Political Economy* vol. 64 (1956) pp. 416–424.

[3] L. Orr, "The Incidence of Differential Property Taxes on Urban Housing," *National Tax Journal* vol. 21 (1968) pp. 253–262.

verified by Oates,[4] Grether and Mieszkowski,[5] and others. That part of the rent of a house which reflects the quality of public services in the community can be regarded as a payment for the public services of that community. Thus, each house in the community earns a rent premium based on the community's provision of public services, and the sum of all of these premiums is the public sector analogue to the revenue received by a private firm for its output.

While the owners of residential property in a community reap the "revenues" of the community's public service production, they also bear the cost of that production through their property taxes. These taxes are set to cover the total costs of public service production. Thus, the net effect of the sum of public service rent premiums minus the sum of tax payments is the "profit" generated by the community from its public service production. As recipients of these profits, the residential property owners of the community are analogous to the stockholders of a firm. The profits of a firm, actual and expected, are capitalized into its market value—that is, the total cost of acquiring complete ownership of the firm. The maximization of profits by a firm is therefore synonymous with the maximization of its market value. So it is with the profits generated by a community's public service production—these profits are capitalized into the market value of houses in the community. Therefore, the community which acts as a private, profit-maximizing firm seeks to provide that combination of public services which maximizes the total value of residential property within its boundaries.

To our knowledge, property value maximization was first set forth as a criterion for local governments by Margolis.[6] Gaffney has also considered it,[7] and Negishi has provided an analysis of its economic implications.[8] Negishi's analysis is weakened, however, by his dependence on a special and unrealistic assumption about consumer preferences.

[4] W. B. Oates, "The Effects of Property Taxes and Public Spending on Property Values: An Empirical Study of Tax Capitalization and the Tiebout Hypothesis," *Journal of Political Economy* vol. 77 (1969) pp. 957–971.

[5] D. M. Grether, and P. Mieszkowski, "Determinants of Real Estate Values," *Journal of Urban Economics* vol. 1 (1974) pp. 127–146.

[6] J. Margolis, "The Demand for Urban Public Services," in H. Perloff and L. Wingo, Jr., eds., *Issues in Urban Economics* (Baltimore, Johns Hopkins University Press for Resources for the Future, 1968).

[7] M. Gaffney, "Tax Reform to Release Land," in M. Clawson, ed., *Modernizing Urban Land Policy* (Baltimore, Johns Hopkins University Press for Resources for the Future, 1973).

[8] T. Negishi, "Public Expenditure Determined by Voting with One's Feet and Fiscal Profitability," *Swedish Journal of Economics* vol. 74 (1972) pp. 452–458.

We believe that it would be beneficial to consider the implications of property value maximization in a more general framework, and it is the objective of this chapter to do so.

THE EFFICIENCY OF PROPERTY VALUE MAXIMIZATION

One reason for our interest in developing a decision criterion for the public sector which is similar to profit maximization in the private sector is that, under the conditions of perfect competition without externalities, profit maximization by private firms leads to overall efficiency in the allocation of resources in the private sector.[9] That is, the result of the self-interested pursuit of profit by private firms is allocationally optimal from the overall standpoint of the private sector. This leads us to ask if the analogue of profit maximization—property value maximization—has the same attractiveness for the local public sector.

We will analyze this possibility, using a simple model of a metropolitan housing market. We will ignore other facets of a single household's consumption choice and concentrate on how it allocates its income between housing and other consumption. To consume more expensive housing, a household must sacrifice expenditures on other consumption and vice versa. Our conclusions about the efficiency of property value maximization will hinge on how each household resolves this tradeoff.

This tradeoff is straightforward for renters because a renter makes a payment each month for his housing. If he is contemplating a move from a dwelling renting for, say, two hundred dollars a month, to one renting for, say, three hundred dollars a month, he will know that he must decrease his expenditures on other consumption by a hundred dollars per month if he moves. Not all leases contain the same provisions concerning which party to the lease is to pay for heat, light, water, etc., but these differences are relatively minor and may be easily costed out to arrive at a rent figure which reflects the relative cost per period of living in one dwelling as opposed to another. We will refer to this adjusted cost per period as the *gross rent* of a dwelling.

[9] Perhaps the clearest demonstration of this proposition can be found in F. Bator, "The Simple Analytics of Welfare Maximization," *American Economic Review* vol. 47 (1957) pp. 22–59.

The tradeoff between housing and other consumption is not as explicit for homeowners as it is for renters. Because a homeowner makes no explicit rental payment each month, it is not clear by how much he must increase or decrease his expenditures per period to rent another dwelling. To establish this tradeoff for the homeowner, we must start with the income side of his budget. If the homeowner were to rent another dwelling and move into it, he could rent his original home and spend this rental income on other consumption. Thus, his income per period— that is, the total amount he can spend on all forms of consumption during a given period—equals the amount he currently spends on other consumption plus the net income his house would earn per period if it were rented out. This net income from his original home, an amount we shall call the *net rent,* is equal to the gross rent which the dwelling would command minus property taxes and maintenance costs. Although this net rent is not actually realized income in the sense that it is money received from an outside source, it is considered a source of income should the homeowner move to another dwelling.

Now, if the net rent of a homeowner's dwelling is considered as income (and it should be), the gross rent which the dwelling would command must be considered as the amount the homeowner is currently spending per period to live in his house. It is his expenditure on housing in the following sense: if he were required to spend any more per period to rent a house, he would have less to spend per period on other consumption than he currently has. This gross rent, then, establishes the tradeoff between housing consumption and other consumption. If the implicit gross rent of a homeowner's house is, say, two hundred dollars a month, and the rent of another house is, say, three hundred dollars a month, he would have to sacrifice one hundred dollars a month of other consumption in order to rent the second house.

Of course, a homeowner has the option of buying another house to live in; he will not necessarily rent a dwelling, as we have argued above, if he moves out of his present dwelling. Similarly, he need not rent his home if he moves out of it; he can also sell it. The possibility of buying instead of renting does not change our system of accounting, however, because the market tends to equilibrate the cost per period of buying a house with the cost per period of renting it. Small deviations in this tendency may be possible due to the differences in risk taking and income tax liability between renting and owning, but these deviations are of no consequence for our model.

By this system of accounting, we are essentially viewing the home-owner in two roles, that of an owner and a consumer. As an owner, he holds a stock of wealth, which includes his home and any other assets he owns. This wealth yields an income; in the case of his home, this income is derived by renting his dwelling to himself at market rates. As a consumer, he allocates this income on housing and other consumption according to his tastes. He counts the gross rent of his home as an expenditure as though he were a renter. In fact, when making decisions about the allocation of their incomes, homeowners and renters are identical. Therefore, we will not distinguish between them in our discussion of the location and consumption decisions of households.

It is important to note that the homeowner-as-consumer pays for his consumption of public services just as renters do—through a higher (implicit) gross rent on his house rather than through property taxes. These taxes are paid by the homeowner acting as an owner and are considered to be a negative entry on the income side of his ledger.

The market value of a dwelling is the capitalized value of its present and future net rents. Assume that P_s is the rent of a particular house in year s, T_s is its tax liability, and M_s is its maintenance costs s years from now. The market value of the dwelling would be

(1)
$$V = \sum_{s=0}^{\infty} \frac{P_s - T_s - M_s}{(1 + r)^s}$$

where r is the rate of interest. Of course, only the rent, tax, and maintenance cost for the present would be known with certainty. In calculating the market value of a house, it is a common assumption that these quantities will remain the same in real terms over the years. Under that assumption, the market value of the house would be

(2)
$$V = \frac{P_o - T_o - M_o}{r}$$

where r is now the real rate of interest. We will adopt this formula for the relationship between the market value of a house and its net rent.

Assume that the metropolitan area under consideration encompasses a large number of communities and an even larger number of dwellings, and that these dwellings differ with respect to their physical characteristics, surroundings, and location. They also differ with respect to the quality of local public services provided by the community in which they are located. A complete description of any dwelling must include all of these factors.

Thus, we represent each house by a value for each of k variables $(x_1, \ldots, x_k)$, where x_1 might be the number of square feet, x_2 might be the distance between the house and the center of the city, and x_3 might be the quality of local police protection, etc.

In principle, we mean this description to be complete in the sense that if any two houses have the same value for each of the k variables which describe them, consumers would not prefer to live in one as opposed to the other. Put another way, no one would be willing to pay more per period to live in one house than he would pay to live in another characterized by identical residential services. Identical dwellings must therefore command the same gross rent. This implies that the gross rent of any dwelling can be written as a function of the residential services that describe it. In this case, let $P(x_1, \ldots, x_k)$ be this function.

The households in the metropolitan area will continuously evaluate the stock of dwellings there with respect to physical characteristics and the public services to which each dwelling provides access. Households must weigh the benefits they would receive from each dwelling with the per period cost of inhabiting it. In considering a dwelling identical to the one the household inhabits, but in a community providing better public services than those to which it currently has access, the household makes this implicit calculation: is the dollar evaluation of the added utility derived from residing in the new community and consuming the improved services greater than the amount of additional rent it would have to pay to live there? The household makes identical calculations for different dwellings within the same community, of course, but in such a case the utility gains would derive from a preferred set of structural characteristics. When each household is residing in its most preferred community and dwelling, no such move is possible. In that case, the marginal benefit of each public service (the amount the household would be willing to pay for an incremental improvement in the quality of any public service) will equal the marginal gross rent associated with that service (the additional gross rent the household would have to pay in an identical dwelling in a new community providing the incremental improvement in the public service).

More formally, we can characterize a typical household as having the utility function $U(c, x_1, \ldots x_g, x_{g+1}, \ldots x_k)$, where c represents expenditures on *all* nonhousing consumption; x_1 through x_g describe the physical characteristics of the dwelling the household inhabits; and x_{g+1} through x_k

are the public services which it consumes by virtue of its residence in a particular community. If the household has a per period income of Y (which includes imputed rent), it will attempt to maximize $U(c, x_1, \ldots, x_g, x_{g+1}, \ldots, x_k)$, subject to the budget constraint $Y - c - P(x_1, \ldots, x_k) \geq O$, where $P(x_1, \ldots, x_k)$ is the gross rent it must pay for the dwelling it inhabits. If the household is maximizing utility with respect to all housing characteristics $x_1, \ldots, x_g$ and all public services $x_{g+1}, \ldots, x_k$, the following must be true:

(3) $$\frac{U_j}{U_c} = P_j \, (j = 1, \ldots, k)$$

where $U_j = \partial U / \partial x_j$ (the marginal utility of an additional unit of x_j), $U_c = \partial U / \partial c$, and $P_j = \partial P(x_1, \ldots, x_k) / \partial x_j$ (the addition to gross rent from an additional unit of x_j). This merely states that no household will occupy a particular dwelling if it can obtain greater net benefit from residing elsewhere.

Let us now consider a representative community in the metropolitan area which is, for the purposes discussed above, attempting to maximize the value of its residential property. It will do so by adjusting its public expenditures to that point at which no increase (decrease) in gross rents due to an increase (decrease) in expenditures is greater than (less than) the increase (decrease) in taxes necessary to keep its budget in balance. This obviously requires a knowledge of the rents which the dwellings in the community will command under any combination of public services that the community might provide. To obtain this information, the community must examine the existing structure of market rents within the metropolitan area. In other words, to determine the rent that dwelling i would command if the community expanded its public services, a dwelling structurally identical to i but located in a community currently producing the contemplated public services would be observed: its current rent would be the expected rent that dwelling i would command if such an expansion of public services was undertaken. To find the total change in gross rents necessitated by an alteration in its public services, the community must obtain this information for each dwelling. When the contemplated mix of services is not currently being produced by another community, the expected gross rents must be determined by interpolation of existing service mixes.

The maximization problem of the community can be formally stated as follows. Suppose a community is composed of n dwellings of various styles. Let P^i be the per period gross rent of dwelling i, T^i be the tax assessed against it, and M^i be the maintenance costs of dwelling i, which we assume to be independent of the community's services. The community balances its budget so that its total tax collections $\sum_{i=1}^{n} T^i$ are equal to F, the total cost of the community's public services. Since the market value of dwelling i can be written as $V^i = P^i - T^i - M^i/r$, the community will maximize

$$(4) \qquad \sum_{i=1}^{n} (P^i - T^i) = \sum_{i=1}^{n} P^i - F$$

It will do so by expending money on each public service until the point is reached where the sum of the increases in gross rents due to an expansion in services is just equal to the cost of the expansion. If we differentiate (see equation 4) with respect to some service, say, x_j, we obtain the following condition for a property value maximizing equilibrium:

$$(5) \qquad \sum_{i=1}^{n} P_j^i = F_j$$

where

$$P_j^i = \frac{\partial P^i}{\partial x_j} \text{ and } F_j = \frac{\partial F}{\partial x_j}$$

If households are maximizing utility and communities are maximizing property values, we can make an even stronger statement. Let U^i represent the utility function of the household occupying dwelling i. From equation 3, $U_j^i/U_c^i = P_j^i$. From equation 5 we know that $\sum_{i=1}^{n} P_j^i = F_j$. Combining both, we can characterize the utility and property value maximizing equilibrium by:

$$(6) \qquad \sum_{i=1}^{n} (U_j^i/U_c^i) = F_j$$

That is, in a full equilibrium the sum of the marginal benefits to the households in the community of an expansion in any public good is equal to its marginal cost. We know from previous studies in welfare economics that this is precisely the condition for the efficient provision of a public good.[10, 11] Therefore, if households make utility maximizing residential choices and if communities maximize property values, resources will be efficiently allocated to the provision of local public services.

[10] H. Bowen, "The Interpretation of Voting in the Allocation of Economic Resources," *Quarterly Journal of Economics* vol. 58 (1943) pp. 27–48.
[11] P. Samuelson, "The Pure Theory of Public Expenditure," *The Review of Economics and Statistics* vol. 36 (1954) pp. 387–389.

Implicit in our demonstration that property value maximization results in an efficient allocation of resources is the assumption that for
every consumer there is a community providing that optimum combination of public services which would equate the consumer's marginal
benefit for each public service with the marginal gross rent of that service. Because of the diversity in consumers' tastes and incomes, however,
this assumption may be impossible to satisfy in practice. At the very
least, it would require a wide variety of public service mixes from which
consumers could make choices. We would expect that the number of
communities required to provide this range of choice would exceed the
number of communities within most metropolitan areas. In that case,
each household would have to settle for the community providing the
quality of each public service which, according to the household's tastes,
most closely approximates its optimum combination of public service
levels. In that community, the household's marginal benefit for each
public service may not be exactly equal to the marginal gross rent of
that service, and consequently, property value maximization may not
lead to efficiency. However, if the metropolitan area is large and if the
communities in that area provide a wide variety of public service mixes,
the equality between marginal benefit and marginal cost will hold approximately for each household. Property value maximization will therefore produce an allocation of resources which is nearly efficient. For
this reason, property value maximization is best suited for large metropolitan areas.

We have characterized a household as being ready to move to any
community whose public services and housing prices are more suited to
its tastes than those of its present community. In reality, the housing
market is very fragmented, and, as a consequence, information about
housing prices and public services may be difficult to acquire. Even if a
household should learn about a community better suited to its tastes
than its present one, it may be reluctant to move there because of the
expense of moving its household possessions and because of brokerage
charges and other costs associated with buying or renting a new home.
As a further impediment to moving, a household, through years of residence in a community, may develop a loyalty and attachment to that
community going beyond its desire to partake in another community's
public services.

When households are maximizing utility in their residential location,
housing prices reflect their public service preferences. The maximization

of property values by communities brings these preferences to bear on the public service production of communities. However, when households fail to reach their utility maximizing residential location because of impediments to moving, these prices do not accurately reflect their preferences, and the maximization of property values may not lead to economic efficiency. Thus, household mobility is an important condition for the proper working of property value maximization.

One measure of the willingness of households to move in response to economic incentives is the percentage of people who actually move during a specific period. According to the U.S. Census, 49 percent of all Americans in metropolitan areas lived in a different house in 1965 than they did in 1970, indicating considerable, if not perfect, mobility.[12] This statistic must be interpreted with caution, however, since the percentage of those who moved indicates not only their willingness to relocate, but also the opportunity to do so. In other words, it also reflects a lack of equilibrium in the metropolitan housing market. Even if all households were perfectly mobile, we would not expect much movement if the housing market were in equilibrium. Thus, the percentage of movers may only partially reflect the degree of household mobility.

Our analysis has concentrated on the local public sector and ignored its private counterpart. In that sense, one might say that property value maximization has been demonstrated to lead to partial efficiency. It is important to keep in mind that partial efficiency is consistent with the goal of overall efficiency, only if all other sectors are operating efficiently. If they are not, imposition of efficiency in one sector may actually lead to a decrease in overall efficiency.

SPILLOVERS AND EXTERNALITIES

Up to this point we have talked as though the public services provided by some community, say A, affect only the value of the dwellings in that community. In reality, the levels of local service provision in one community may affect property values in neighboring and, in some cases, spatially distinct communities. In large metropolitan areas, we may expect such "spillovers," as they are called, to be the rule rather than the exception.

[12] U.S. Census for 1970, *Mobility for States and the Nation.*

The reason we must be concerned with the effects of A's public services on property values in other communities is that these spillovers can prevent property value maximization from leading to an efficient allocation of resources in the public sector. In the absence of spillovers, we have seen that community A will, by maximizing $\sum_{i\epsilon A} P^i - F^A$ (the sum of the gross rents earned by the properties in A minus the total cost of the public services provided), produce each service to the point where the sum of the property owners' marginal valuations of an additional unit of that service equals the marginal cost of the added unit.

To see how spillovers will prevent the efficient provision of public services, consider an increase in community A's provision of police protection, which takes the form of an additional hourly patrol of each street in A. If we assume that such patrols deter crime, property values in A will appreciate and, in an attempt to maximize property values, A will expand police patrols to that point at which $\sum_{i\epsilon A} P_j{}^i = F_j{}^A$ (where police protection is the jth public service). However, these patrols may well deter crime along the streets which border community A as well. In so doing, the patrols increase the values of those properties in other communities along the border streets. For an efficient allocation of resources to police protection, these increases in property values in communities other than A must be taken into account: all benefits must be counted, regardless of to whom they accrue. In other words, police protection should be provided to that point where

(7) $$\sum_{i\epsilon A} P_j{}^i + \sum_{i\notin A} P_j{}^i = F_j{}^A,$$

the second sum representing the appreciation of property values in communities B, C, etc., as a result of A's increased patrols.

Therefore, a community which seeks to maximize only the value of the property within its boundaries will tend to provide too little of those services that increase property values elsewhere. Besides police protection, we can easily imagine benefits spilling over from one community to others with respect to fire protection (since neighboring communities often assist each other on multialarm fires), parks and recreation, education, or pollution abatement.

In fact, publicly provided education and the cost of pollution abatement raise still another problem with property value maximization. While it is true that one community's expenditures for police and fire protection or recreation may benefit other nearby or contiguous communities (and in a way that is measurable), this is probably not the case with education or, perhaps, pollution abatement. The benefits from the local provision of these services may be so spread across large metropolitan areas and beyond that they will not be reflected in property values. In the case of education, citizens everywhere benefit from an informed and educated electorate; moreover, all the firms in a metropolitan area benefit from a highly skilled and educated labor force. With respect to pollution control, meteorological conditions in an area may be such that airborne or waterborne residuals are widely diffused. While people all across a metropolitan area, or along an entire river basin, may benefit from community A's expenditure on pollution abatement, these benefits may not be reflected in property values.

In such cases, grants from county or state governments, or even the federal government, may be required to induce these local communities to produce optimal levels of local public services. This is, of course, one of the reasons behind state and federal aid to public schools and federal subsidies for the construction of local waste treatment plants.

There is another reason for these transfers, however, which also bears on property value maximization as a decision criterion for local governments. When communities provide public services to maximize local property values, they are, as we have pointed out, selling these services through housing prices and are guided in their production decisions by property value changes. However, many feel that education, health, and safety are services to which all citizens have a right regardless of their ability to buy them either directly in private markets or indirectly through housing markets. If the well-being of most citizens depends upon the provision of such services to those who could not otherwise afford them, property value maximization would again lead to an underprovision of those services. It is for the increased provision of such services that grants are also directed.

In summary, when certain services provide spillover benefits to neighboring communities (which may or may not be reflected in property value changes) or when these services are considered to be the basic rights of all citizens, intergovernmental grants will be required to stimulate local public service provision beyond the property value maximizing levels.

PROBLEMS OF EQUITY

Within a particular community, property value maximization cannot be expected to have identical effects on the values of all dwellings. This has important implications for its political feasibility. To better understand this, suppose that a community is providing less than the property value maximizing level of education. If the community were to increase expenditures to that level, by definition, the total value of property in the community would increase. However, this increase may take the form of increases in the value of all dwellings or it may result from increases in the value of certain dwellings that are large enough to offset declines in the values of others.[13] If few dwellings appreciate when property values are maximized and many others decline in value, property value maximization may encounter considerable political opposition. This is less likely to be the case if most dwellings appreciate when total property value is maximized.

To see how this is possible, we must first observe that the distribution among dwellings of an increase in total property values depends upon the distributions of gross rents and taxes. Both are determined by the housing market—directly so in the case of gross rents and indirectly in regard to property taxes in the sense that market values form the basis for their assessment. Suppose, for example, that an increase in educational expenditures increases the gross rent of each dwelling by the same percentage, say, 3 percent. The ratio of the gross rent of any particular dwelling to the total gross rent earned by all dwellings would therefore remain constant. This would in turn imply that the tax share of each dwelling would remain constant,[14] and the tax bill for each would increase by the same proportion, say, 1 percent (if we assume that the expenditure increase has a positive net effect on property values). With

---

[13] Let us again emphasize that houses which decline in value do so because the increase in their gross rent is more than offset by the increase in their property tax liability—it is this net effect which can be negative.

[14] To see this, let α^i = the tax share of dwelling i, v^i = the market value of dwelling i; $V = \sum_i v^i$; p^i = the gross rent of dwelling i; t^i = the per period taxes on i; $P = \sum P^i$; $T = \sum t^i$; and r = the rate of interest. Then,

$$\alpha^i = \frac{v^i}{V} = \frac{(p^i - t^i)/r}{(P - T)/r} = \frac{p^i - \alpha^i T}{P - T}$$

Therefore,

$$\alpha^i(P - T) = p^i - \alpha^i T \text{ and } \alpha^i = p^i/P$$

If p^i increases by x percent for all i, each α^i will obviously remain constant.

the gross rents of each dwelling increasing by 3 percent, while property taxes are increasing by 1 percent, each dwelling would increase in value by 2 percent.

In general, gross rents will *not* increase in the same proportion when the level of a public service is altered. Certain dwelling styles may be scarce relative to others, and the gross rents of these dwellings will be higher, reflecting that scarcity. When gross rents change disproportionately, so do tax shares. It would therefore be possible for the market values of certain dwellings to go up while the value of others is falling. Given the existing property tax system, then, property value maximization may not command much support.

Some houses may fail to share in total property value increases because the current tax system does not allocate increments in taxes on the basis of increments in gross rents. Such a tax system might work as follows. First, a certain level of expenditure for each public service would be specified and each dwelling in the community would be taxed to pay for these services. For any change in expenditures from this established level, tax increments would be assigned to each house in proportion to its change in gross rent. If the change in gross rent for a particular house is represented by Δp, its change in taxes would be $c\Delta p$; where c, as a factor of proportionality, is the same for all houses in the community. This factor of proportionality would be set so as to change total taxes by the amount required to balance the new budget. If ΔT represents the total change in taxes required and ΔP is the total change in gross rents, c can be set so that $\Delta T = c\Delta P$. So long as the change in gross rents exceeds the change in taxes, the value of each house increases in proportion to its change in gross rent. This would work both for increases and decreases in expenditures.

The current use of betterment taxes is a precedent for this incremental tax system. A betterment is an improvement that adds to the value of a property, and for our purposes here, it is the result of some governmental action such as public works. A betterment tax is designed to capture this increase through levying a tax on the improved land. According to Grimes,[15] betterment taxes have been or are now being used in Latin America, India, Indonesia, Israel, Denmark, Italy, and the

---

[15] O. Grimes, *Urban Land and Public Policy: Social Appropriation and Betterment,* International Bank for Reconstruction and Development Staff Working Paper No. 179 (Washington, D.C., IBRD, 1974).

United Kingdom. Although betterment taxes are similar (in their manner of assessing tax liability) to the incremental tax system we have outlined, their objective is different. A betterment tax aims to appropriate the total private gain from publicly financed improvements, while our proposed incremental tax system is aimed only at distributing the cost of public improvements in proportion to the benefits they generate.

We have not indicated how a *status quo* point might be selected for this incremental tax system. It would certainly be possible to set a community's current situation as its *status quo*. As property value-maximizing expenditure changes occur, the tax system would tend to preserve this original distribution of property values.

The community could take a longer-run view, however. Because of some notion about the public cost of growth alternatives, a community might wish to encourage the construction of certain housing types over others. By giving those types a property tax break at the *status quo* point, the market values of these dwellings would be higher than normal, thereby encouraging their construction. Once the initial tax distribution was settled, total property values could be maximized without altering the favorable status of these housing types. This incremental tax system allows the community to pursue a long-term growth policy while it continues to make expenditure decisions on the basis of property value maximization.

Our proposed incremental tax-share system has one obvious advantage when compared with the present method of financing changes in the levels of public service provision. Under the current fixed-tax-share system, referenda on proposed increases in public services can be carried by a majority, no matter how small. This often results in large numbers of dissatisfied resident-voters, many of whom seem never to "win" in such elections. In theory, at least, our scheme of incremental taxation would eliminate this problem. Since each resident's tax increase would depend upon his share of the increased benefits (as measured by increases in the value of his dwelling), and since only efficient proposals would be undertaken, each dwelling owner would benefit by every proposed alteration in his community's public services. There would, therefore, be a unanimity of opinion on each proposed change, proving a pleasant contrast to the rancor which follows a particularly close referendum under the current system. In the discussion which follows, we will cover the workability of such a scheme.

TABLE 3-1. Percentage of Households Owning Their Own Homes, July 1971

Annual household income (in dollars)	Percentage
Under 3,000	49.9
3,000–4,999	54.5
5,000–7,999	55.4
7,500–9,999	65.8
10,000–14,999	76.1
15,000 and over	85.1

Source: U.S. Department of Commerce, *Consumer Buying Indicators* no. 40 (Washington, D.C.: Govt. Print. Off., May 1972) p. 25.

We have discussed the distribution of gains between the property owners in the community, but there is a broader distributional question to consider. On its face, property value maximization tends to further the economic interests of homeowners in general. Since homeowners tend to be wealthier as a group than renters, as table 3-1 indicates, property value maximization may tend to aggravate an already inequitable distribution of wealth. For this reason, it might be argued that property value maximization promotes efficiency at the expense of equity.

The same argument could be made about profit maximization by private firms, however. The ownership of such firms tends to be concentrated among the wealthy, and hence an increase in profits in the private sector has a detrimental effect on the distribution of wealth. Many people who share this view about the inequity of the current wealth distribution still think firms ought to maximize profits, however. This view is based on the belief that an adequate degree of redistribution can be achieved through the federal tax system without seriously distorting incentives for economic efficiency. It is argued that the efficient operation of the economy need not, and thus should not, be sacrificed because of the desire to achieve a more equitable distribution of wealth.

For these same reasons, efficiency in the provision of public services by local governments need not be sacrificed. Attempts at income redistribution within a community tend to be self-defeating anyway. A policy designed to increase the income of a community's poor serves mainly to drive out those wealthy citizens who must pay for it, a point made by Oates among others.[16] It would be better, it seems to us, to aim for income redistribution on a national level and to concentrate on efficiency at the local level.

PROPERTY VALUE MAXIMIZATION IN PRACTICE

Surprisingly, perhaps, we conclude that property value maximization could be practiced quite easily if two requirements were met. First, highly detailed records must be kept of the sales prices and the structural characteristics of all dwellings sold in our sample metropolitan area. Second, adequate measures of each of the public services provided by the communities within the area must be developed.

These two requirements are essential to the applicability of property value maximization because, as we have pointed out, the price of a house depends upon the mix of public services provided by the community in which it is located, as well as on its physical or structural characteristics. Detailed information on both allows us to estimate the amount contributed to the gross rent of a dwelling from each physical characteristic and each local public service. This can be accomplished by statistical regression, using as observations each of the houses sold in the metropolitan area in a single time period. Each observation would consist of the gross rent of the house, say, P_1, a vector of the structural characteristics of the house, say, $x_{11}, \ldots, x_{1j}$,[17] and a vector of the public service outputs of the community in which the dwelling is located, say, $x_{1,j+1}, \ldots, x_{1k}$. (The gross rent of a house can be calculated from its sales price.) If there were, for example, n houses sold in the metropolitan area during our chosen time period, we could array our observations in the following way:

$$
\begin{bmatrix}
P_1 & x_{11} \ldots x_{1j} & x_{1,j+1} \ldots x_{1k} \\
\cdot & & \\
\cdot & & \\
\cdot & & \\
P_n & x_{n1} \ldots x_{nj} & x_{n,j+1} \ldots x_{nk}
\end{bmatrix}
$$

By regressing the gross rent on these structural characteristics and public services, we could, for example, determine the effect on the gross

[16] W. Oates, *Fiscal Federalism* (New York, Harcourt Brace Jovanovich, 1972).
[17] Where x_{ij} is interpreted as the jth characteristic of the ith dwelling.

rent of a house that its number of rooms, a sunporch, finished basement, copper plumbing, or a slate roof may have.

Even more important for our purposes are the estimated effects of local public services on the gross rent of dwellings, since this is the information which communities in the area would use as a guide in their production decisions. For example, the regression equation would indicate by how much the value of a particular dwelling with a given set of structural characteristics would appreciate should the community in which it was located increase its expenditures on parks and recreation, public works, police protection, or public education.

The reliability of the regression coefficients quite obviously depends upon the accuracy of the measures of structural characteristics and local public services. The former present little conceptual difficulty, since assessors currently record information on many of the structural characteristics of the dwellings. Such data should become even more comprehensive and accurate as additional states and localities follow the lead of those that have begun to implement computerized assessment; for example, California and New York are the two states currently most committed to the concept, and several other states are exploring the idea. Furthermore, the recording of detailed structural information could easily be made a requirement of deed transfer.

The measurement of local public service output presents a more formidable problem, however. Quite obviously, it is less difficult to determine the square footage of a living room than it is to measure the quality of police protection in a community or to rank elementary schools on the basis of their "output." While we do not suggest that perfectly acceptable measures of all local services are at hand, we do feel that the information required to construct such measures is slowly becoming available. In addition to the familiar expenditure-per-capita measure of the output of various services, new measures include the use of aggregate and specific crime rates for police department output, fire insurance company ratings and the number and types of fires for fire department output, the number of recreational functions performed and park acreage statistics as measures of recreation departments, and total book stock, circulation, volumes per capita, and information desk referrals for measures of local public library output.

Education merits special attention because it is the publicly provided service most influencing residential property values. In addition, it is perhaps the most difficult service to measure. If the quality of education can be measured by expenditure per pupil, this problem is made much less difficult. Such a measure may be appropriate if parents are interested in their childrens' presence in uncrowded, modern, well-equipped schools apart from the effects which such conditions could be expected to have on more concrete measures such as reading scores and progress, or Iowa test and IQ scores. In such a case, parents would be purchasing expenditures per pupil as a final consumption good. Alternatively, if studies on the "production" of education pin down the contribution of expenditures per pupil to improved test scores or other output measures, expenditures per pupil may be used as an indirect measure of the school quality. At any rate, the production and measurement of educational output is being given considerable attention by economists, educators, and others, and we may hope for better, if not definitive, measures when these studies are completed.

What we are trying to suggest is that property value maximization is not at all infeasible as a practical criterion. As a final bit of evidence to support this point, let us describe briefly some work which we have begun in this direction. The San Mateo County (California) assessor has supplied us with information on the structural characteristics and sales prices of homes sold in that county in 1970, and we have constructed various measures of the public services provided by each of the communities in the county. Using these, we can estimate a gross rent equation such as the one discussed above. This equation can be used to estimate the increases in the gross rent of each of the single-family dwellings in the South San Francisco Unified and Ravenswood school districts, resulting from the passage of school tax referenda held in the respective districts in 1970. By comparing these expected increases in gross rent with the increases in property taxes, which would have been assessed against each dwelling if the referenda passed, we can determine what the expected net effect of the proposed change in school spending would have been on each dwelling.

These estimated net effects are important for the following reason: while studies of voter participation and outcomes in local school tax referenda number well over one hundred, none has used as an explanatory variable the net fiscal effects which we are calculating. That is, no one has considered the possibility that a property owner may vote for an increase in educational expenditures if the proposed increase will raise his gross rent by more than his tax liability and that he will oppose the change otherwise. By combining our estimates of the expected net effect of an increase in the community's educational expenditures with the actual precinct voting returns in the two elections which were held, we intend to test the hypothesis that citizens vote to maximize property values. We hope to report the results of this part of our research in the near future. We mention it here only to point out that it should be theoretical rather than practical objections which prevent the adoption of property value maximization for the public service production decisions of local communities.

CONCLUSION

It is clear that our overall assessment of property value maximization depends upon the relative strengths and weaknesses we have discussed. That property value maximization would lead to the efficient allocation of resources in the local public sector is highly significant. Let us restate the importance of this point: at a time when the financial resources of most local governments are being severely strained, property value maximization would ensure that no reallocation of resources from one service to another could improve the economic welfare of one household without worsening that of another. In other words, no allocation of resources, other than that which maximizes property values, produces as great a total of economic benefits.

The drawbacks to property value maximization are of course very real. Perhaps the most serious of these are the impediments to household mobility. The range of public service mixes available in a metropolitan area may indeed be too narrow, although we would expect this range to increase with the size of the area. The high economic costs of moving and acquiring information can perhaps be combated, the latter through a publication containing information about crime rates, school quality, average rental values, housing prices, etc., in each of the communities in the metropolitan area. The biggest barrier to mobility may well be the "psychic" costs of leaving a neighborhood or friends in a community to which households feel loyal. These loyalties cause households to value their dwellings more highly than the market values them and, therefore, reduce significantly the household's mobility.

Next, public services provided by one community will often affect property values in neighboring communities, or they may generate external benefits all across a metropolitan area which are not fully or even partially reflected in property values. As we have pointed out, in the presence of such effects property value maximization will lead to suboptimal levels of public services. Also, society has expressed a preference for the provision of certain "merit" goods like health and education to all individuals, regardless of their ability to pay for these services in private markets or through the housing market. Property value maximization would not value these merit needs beyond their contributions to gross rents.

Nevertheless, we have tried to indicate that these problems are not insurmountable; moreover, their solution need not require a sacrifice of the apparent efficiency of property value maximization. In the case of spillover benefits, the widespread system of intergovernmental grants could be extended to encourage the expansion by communities of those services generating such benefits. In fact, communities could finance their grants to other spillover-generating communities by taxes levied only against those residents whose property values are enhanced by the spillovers. This would be an application of our incremental taxation scheme. As for the provision of certain services to lower-income residents, we would reemphasize that transfers of income through a negative income tax or similar scheme, handled at the federal level so as not to encourage avoidance by the wealthy, would be much more effective. Such transfers would allow low-income residents to purchase badly needed services either privately or through the housing market. It would have the considerable advantage of noninterference with what we have suggested is an efficiently operating market for local public services.

4 / MARK F. SHAREFKIN

Metropolitan Growth and the Public Utilities

PROVISION OF PUBLIC UTILITY SERVICES: OLD VERSUS NEW ISSUES

THE PUBLIC UTILITY SERVICES—electricity, water and sewerage, and transport—are subject to direct regulation because their provision has long been recognized as affecting the public interest. As such, the circumstances of their production and consumption have been the subjects of public controversy and have intrigued welfare-minded students of the public sector.

But there has been a dramatic change in the kinds of issues raised in respect to the public utility services. In the past, the issues were essentially ones of efficiency: given a persuasive rationale for public provision or regulation of one or another of these services, the problem was how to efficiently utilize and allocate resources to the service in question.

No longer are we concerned only with questions of efficient delivery of public services. Now a vast array of issues faces the regulatory agencies. For example, the public utility services are central to problems of environmental management, and environmental constraints have been a major concern of regulatory hearings on electricity, water and sewerage, and transport. Much more than an addendum to the regulatory agenda, these concerns have powerfully affected the framework in which even the traditional rate and investment decision items are discussed. At one

The author is a senior research associate, Resources for the Future.

level are the now familiar environmental impact issues associated with public services: for example, air and thermal pollution with electricity generation, water quality with sewerage and water treatment, and air quality and noise levels with transportation. These problems would occur even in a world where no new power plants were built and population and industrial output remained unchanged. At another and more vexing level are problems intimately connected with rapid changes in consumption patterns, metropolitan populations, and metropolitan areas themselves. These include the alleged growth biases of existing pricing and investment practices and institutions and, also, problems surrounding the conscious use of utility pricing and investment policies as planning instruments for the direction of metropolitan growth toward desired ends. The current issues raise questions about the adequacy and legitimacy of our regulatory institutions: Are they capable of making public service pricing and investment decisions? What is their relationship to elected government officials and to the firms they regulate?

ANALYZING THE NEW ISSUES: THE SEARCH FOR A METHOD

Economists have formulated an impressive apparatus for dealing with the older efficiency issues. But, in regard to the newer questions, their performance has not been exceptional. In part this is their fault, for they have not mastered the tools that are now needed. The explanation for this marginal success also partly stems from the new issues themselves— their pervasiveness and resistance to categorization and organization. Consider, as an example of our shortsightedness, the tools we have at hand for dealing with allegations that the pricing of some of the utilities services leads to "sprawl," that is, to inefficiently large urban areas. Analyses of the welfare consequences of metropolitan size and distribution are in their infancy. Moreover, the tractable general equilibrium models of metropolitan location are overly simplistic,[1] and their conclusions are very sensitive to the particular assumptions required to formulate tractable models. As an example of the difficulty of improvement

---

[1] See, for example, the summary of E. Mills and J. MacKinnon, "Notes on the New Urban Economics," *Bell Journal of Economics and Management Science* vol. 4, no. 2 (Autumn 1973) p. 593.

here, consider the well-known problems associated with the complexity of location decisions in the urban area. If the proximity-related externality interactions are included, serious difficulties of principle arise.[2] On the other hand, if these interactions are omitted, the whole exercise is of questionable realism.

METHODS OF THE STUDY

The analytical implications of these observations for the new issues in public utility service regulation seem clear, if unsettling, especially those concerned with metropolitan growth. The new issues, though an identifiable area of study, are not necessarily an identifiable area of analysis. That is, they are not susceptible to a single method or paradigm; instead an eclectic approach is required in which tools and procedures are borrowed or fashioned as needed by the subproblem being modeled or the issue being discussed. Further, while there are important similarities in cost structures, demand patterns, and technologies among the metropolitan public utilities, there are equally important differences. Though there are obvious economies in fully exploiting their similarities, their differences suggest that some issues are of more importance to one service than to another. In such cases, I will use a particular service to make a particular point.

Generally, when studying the regulated industries, a disproportionate amount of attention is paid to the regulatory process itself, while the particular characteristics of the regulated industries are neglected. This has occurred in some studies of public utility provision, and, in an attempt to avoid this problem, I will begin with an overview of each of the public utility services—electricity, water and sewerage, and transport— in a metropolitan setting. Here, as elsewhere in the chapter, many examples will be drawn from the Washington, D.C., SMSA, probably the most overstudied area in the nation. There are other examples as well, particularly prominent court cases, and, where dependable sources of comparable data and cross-sectional studies of communities exist, these, too, have been used.

---

[2] The classic demonstration of this is that of T. C. Koopmans and M. Beckmann, "Assignment Problems and the Location of Economic Activity," *Econometrica* vol. 25, no. 1 (January 1957) p. 53.

Following the initial overview, the issues and questions raised therein are discussed further, with emphasis being placed upon a method, procedure, or example that illuminates, focuses, or provides the framework for empirical simulation modeling and resolution of one of the cited issues. Throughout the issues sections, I have attempted to integrate the social choice questions with the traditional economic questions. In each case, I have tried to answer the following questions: How have the new issues revealed the weaknesses and limitations of traditional public service pricing and investment procedures? How have traditional pricing and investment procedures been changed to accommodate the new issues and concerns? And, under some reasonable and explicit normative standards, has this modification been good or bad?

THE PUBLIC UTILITIES IN A METROPOLITAN CONTEXT

Rationales for Regulation

The public utilities in question are electricity, water and sewerage, and transport. All are supplied, in part or in full, by public authorities and are under regulatory constraints. Their public utility status is based on the traditional rationales of increasing returns to scale (or decreasing costs) and the presence of a peak-load problem (that is, because demand varies much more rapidly than capacity can be adjusted to meet demand, the costs of storage are prohibitive). These three services are relatively capital intensive. Therefore, over and above the peak-load problem, there is the longer-term concern with matching future capacity to future demand when demand is known only uncertainly. This means planning in an uncertain environment, with very high penalty costs for incorrect decisions. Particularly relevant to the provision of these services in a metropolitan area is the physical distribution system linking consumers with generating and treatment facilities or their destinations. For a comparison of public service technologies, see table 4-1.

However, these generalities do not come to grips with the specific features of these technologies that are most pertinent to the new issues, and they do not begin to answer the challenges directed toward the traditional rationales themselves. Thus, for each of the public utility services, it is necessary to have some understanding of (1) the cost structures under which that service is provided, (2) rule-of-thumb prac-

TABLE 4-1. Comparison of Public Utility Service Technologies

Service/phase	Generation	Transmission	Distribution
Water	Collection at reservoirs or from surface water or groundwater	Piping, with gravity flow or pumping or both, where sources are distant	Metropolitan distribution system piping
Sewerage	Wastewater treatment	Pumping, through interceptor and then trunkline sewers, to treatment plant	Collection from population centers
Electricity	Generation at power plants	Transmission system lines	Distribution system lines
Intrametropolitan (commuting) transportation	Centers of employment and population	Limited access highways and mass transit rail right-of-way	Local (unlimited access) roads and collector public transport systems

tices for setting rates and expanding capacity, and (3) the way in which the new issues are tied to these practices.

Water and Sewerage

Here, it is helpful to distinguish the several phases by which water is delivered, and sewage removed, from places of use and disposal in metropolitan areas. First, water must be brought from some distant source; and if it becomes necessary to exploit successively even more distant surface water sources, there will be long-run increasing costs in bringing water into the metropolitan area. Even where local groundwater sources exist, higher pumping rates will make it necessary to pump from lower groundwater levels, so that future costs will be higher here as well.

If it is necessary to treat the water before its distribution to tap points, there are likely to be economies of scale—long-run decreasing costs—in treatment. Finally, there is the distribution system linking the water treatment plant with consumption points. This system is generally characterized by long-run *decreasing* costs and short-run *increasing* costs. The decreasing costs have a geometric basis: the ratio of the circumference of a pipe to its cross-sectional area decreases as the reciprocal of the radius, so that both the capital costs of pipe installation and the circumferential drag on throughput, which imposes operating (pumping) costs, decrease per unit of throughput volume at a given pumping velocity. The actual design of a pumping system will take advantage of gravity flow in order to economize on pumping costs; but the geometric facts are immutable.

At any given time, the considerable capital investment in any of the metropolitan public utilities is allocated among users by some mix of price- and nonprice-rationing devices; and at any given time, by virtue of the depreciation of past investment, public utility service capital in place is changing the process of investment in new equipment for all phases of production and delivery, as well as effecting changes in other service dimensions, such as the number and location of customers.

In both pricing and investment, the diversity of practices among jurisdictions within and across metropolitan areas is substantial. Though normative rules for pricing and investment are necessarily intertwined, it is probably best, for our purposes here, to discuss pricing and investment practices separately.

Pricing of water and sewerage services. The diversity in pricing practices is enormous: some cities, such as New York, finance residential water services out of general revenues; others, such as Washington, D.C., charge for water use.[3] Nevertheless, the American Water Works Association's Water Rates Manual is a nationally recognized guide for "best-practice" water and sewerage rate-making.[4] Although there is now no unanimity among water authorities and companies, the prestige of the AWWA makes adherence to its recommendations a possibility for the future. Its rate recommendations are a good starting point when discussing pricing practices general enough to be applicable to many U.S. water and sewerage utilities.

[3] The classic treatment of the way in which choices between general and specific financing should be made is that of W. Vickrey, "General and Specific Financing of Urban Services," in Howard G. Schaller, ed., *Public Expenditure Decisions in the Urban Community* (Baltimore, Johns Hopkins University Press for Resources for the Future, 1963). Needless to say, the actual decision-making process is quite different, probably unfortunately so.

[4] American Water Works Association, *Water Rates Manual* (1960), as reprinted from *Journal of the American Water Works Association*, vol. 46, no. 3 (March 1954). See the critique of this manual in J. Hirshleifer, J. DeHaven, and M. Milliman, *Water Supply: Economics, Technology, and Policy* (Chicago, University of Chicago Press, 1960) pp. 88–113.

The AWWA rate design recommendations are based on a "revenue requirement," a standard first step in the determination of utility rates. It recommends either the standard fair return on rate base or cash basis determinations,[5] with rate structures then designed to yield that required revenue. The relationship between this revenue requirement and the various financial measures of cost depends upon a prior decision, the mix of financing between general revenues and user charges. An "incorrect" choice of this mix means that the whole rate determination will proceed from a faulty financial cost measurement. It is not my intention to sum up the extensive literature on this problem;[6] two somewhat obvious determinants of the financing decision are relevant to the discussion. Any utility department or commission with growth objectives will be biased toward general financing, since customers can then be served at prices below cost, while output is expanded. A financially strained municipality may seek to operate services—such as water and sewerage—for which charges are based on a fiscal surplus, with "diversion" of that surplus into the general fisc. Some jurisdictions have sought to circumvent this problem by severing the financing of water or sewerage services or both from the general fisc. This, however, does not eliminate the first problem.

Subsequent to this determination of revenue requirement, the AWWA's recommended procedures for rate-structural design begin with a distinction between special and normal customers. Special customers are those "whose maximum demand, in relation to the average, is higher than normal because of seasonal or intermittent use."[7] Examples of special use include water for fire protection, air conditioning and refrigeration, lawn sprinkling, golf courses, other irrigation needs, and "certain commercial and industrial" uses. Thus, the line between special and normal users is drawn by selecting a cutoff value of noncoincident load factor—the ratio of maximum demand to average demand. All uses above that line are classified as "special," and all uses below that line are "normal." This distinction is the recommended basis for allocation of capacity costs between the two kinds of customers. The manual suggests that total capacity costs be allocated between special and normal customers, but it does not suggest a single, best-allocation rule.

[5] The rationales and limitations of these procedures are discussed in detail in A. E. Kahn, *The Economics of Regulation* (New York, Wiley, 1970).
[6] See Vickrey, "General and Specific Financing of Urban Services."
[7] American Water Works Association, *Water Rates Manual*, p. 13.

Given the allocation of total capacity costs between special and normal customers, the AWWA recommends that total special customer capacity costs be allocated among individual special customer subclasses in proportion to the ratio of the customer's (or customer's subclass) noncoincident demand to the total noncoincident demand.

The allocation of capacity costs is the first step in setting special customer rates. The stages of the typical regulatory rate-making procedure include the following:

1. Determination of revenue requirement
2. Determination of rate structures
3. Assignment of all customer classes
4. Allocation of capacity costs to customer classes
5. Allocation of operating and maintenance costs to customer classes
6. Design of rate structures for each customer class.

Each stage has its particular institutional mechanics, which will be explored below. Thus far we have traced the AWWA's water rate recommendations through the identification of distinct customer classes and the allocation of system capacity costs among those customer classes. The allocation of operating and maintenance costs among customer classes is much simpler. These costs are roughly proportional to customer consumption and can be allocated in proportion to customer class consumption.[8]

Next, customer class rates—the formulas for computing individual bills of all customers in a specific customer class—must be determined. Traditional rate-making doctrine has held that revenues raised from a specific customer class should cover the fully allocated costs of service to that group. For the water utility's special customers, the AWWA recommends that capacity costs be assigned in proportion to the customer's share in noncoincident maximum special customer class demand, and that those capacity costs be recovered in lump sum charges—either by meter rent or minimum bill charges. It is also suggested that operating and maintenance costs be assigned in proportion to water consumption; thus, the recommended commodity rate for special customers is a flat rate.

Turning to the manual for normal customer rates, four bases for rate design are suggested, but not ranked or compared:

[8] Ibid., p. 32.

1. A demand basis for normal users, with a graduated meter rent for each successively larger-sized meter, and commodity rates in three steps. Included in, and recovered from, the meter rent would be general and administrative costs, metering costs for normal users, and a demand charge equal to 50 percent of the fixed costs. Under this proposal, commodity rates would be imposed in three or four steps, or rate blocks, with the block lengths based on the AWWA's 1923 rate schedule,[9] and the block height based upon arbitrarily selected numerical ratios—for example, 2 to 1 between the first and third blocks and not more than 3 to 1 between the first and fourth blocks.

2. A functional cost basis for normal users, with customer costs embedded in a minimum bill and demand costs embedded in the commodity charge, with the latter being determined in the same way as for the demand basis.

3. Finally, the manual lists (without recommendation) two rate structures as potentially applicable to both special and normal customers. First, commodity rates only, with special uses charged separately to special customers, and with a minimum charge assessed against all normal users. And, second, commodity rates only, but with a minimum charge sufficient to cover the costs of all special users.[10]

What are the properties of these rate structures? How do they depart from the normative efficiency standard of public utility pricing theory? Have these departures allowed room for the exercise of discretion—by public water utilities, municipal water authorities, and regulatory commissions—in cost allocation? And which of these departures are likely to be especially significant in their impact upon patterns of metropolitan location, and in their distributional implications?

First, the AWWA's recommended water rate structures make no attempt to reflect distribution cost differentials in locationally differentiated water prices. The classification of customers into homogeneous customer classes is based upon load characteristics alone—the time pattern of demand—and not upon the costs of delivering that service to different

---

[9] In general these recommendations have been followd by water utilities but, more accurately, they are typical of all utilities.

[10] American Water Works Association, *Water Rates Manual*, p. 25.

customers.[11] The only portion of the manual explicitly concerned with intraclass, spatial cost differentials deals not with costs and pricing but with the revenue requirement calculation. It recommends that rates charged suburban areas by municipal utilities be computed on the basis of the so-called utility or fair return on fair value,[12] in such a way that those rates,

if applied to all users, would provide for the operation and maintenance expense, plus local taxes, depreciation and a reasonable return on the value of all property devoted to the common service of the entire area . . . but excluding the . . . facilities provided for serving areas within the city. The sum of all such costs divided by the total annual production, less transmission losses, given an average wholesale price . . . applicable to all outside areas. . . . On such a theory, if the utility basis is used inside the city . . . there is no difference between city and suburban rates, except for charges that may be justified as extra costs in particular situations.

This recommendation is consistent with, but need not imply, the reflection of spatial cost of service differentials in water rates. A city-suburban differential rate, which may or may not be an improvement over a single rate for the combined areas, meets the manual's requirements, and spatial differentiation will depend upon the fortunate accident of distinct jurisdictions in city and suburb. In practice, this possibility is a real problem, for the allocation of distribution capacity costs often depends markedly upon the jurisdiction's boundaries.

Second, and perhaps of less importance for water than for the other public utility services, is the allocation of capacity costs among special users in proportion to noncoincident demand. The line of causality in cost incurrence runs from coincident demand at peak—on the "maximum day," the day upon which water use is highest—to capacity cost; noncoincident demand is irrelevant as a determinant of imposed capacity cost. It is sometimes argued, in defense of noncoincident demand pricing, that if customer classes have been properly defined, so that load patterns within customer classes are fairly homogeneous, the administrative and metering costs saved by charging capacity costs on a noncoincident basis may exceed the gains from coincident demand pricing.

[11] Ibid., p. 6.
[12] In this sense two of the three public utility services—water and sewerage and interurban transportation—are very different from electricity, the third. For the former two the role of federal subsidies in investment is crucial.

But for very large users that is rarely the case. The explanations for failure to charge on a coincident demand basis may lie elsewhere, perhaps, in institutional arrangements.

Investment of water and sewerage service capital. In the discussion of the AWWA's recommendations for water and sewerage pricing, it was noted that the AWWA did not offer a solution to the problem of recovering the different costs of service imposed by customers in different locations. The manual's recommendations refer only to that portion of costs which must be covered by the utility; but in sewerage a major federal subsidy is available for local investment in water treatment and interceptor sewer piping capacity.[13] Under the Federal Water Pollution Control Amendments of 1972, the Environmental Protection Agency (EPA) is obligated to fund 75 percent of the capital costs of all interceptor sewers and collection systems found eligible under the relevant statutes; this general financing represents an extension of the previous and continuing provisions of the act for EPA funding of 75 percent of wastewater treatment plant construction costs. These subsidies have been based on water pollution rationales. Federal subsidies are required because the benefits of sewage treatment do not all accrue to the jurisdiction paying the treatment costs; for example, an upstream jurisdiction would have no incentive to treat sewage which affected only downstream jurisdictions. The effectiveness of such federal intervention has not been proved as yet,[14] since little incentive is provided for private abatement efforts, and because subsidization of capital costs alone does not help jurisdictions which cannot meet operating costs. Other unintended consequences of the federal program have received relatively less attention. In particular, possible distortions of locational and land use decisions are nowhere reckoned as program costs;[15] and the federal subsidy reinforces spatially undifferentiated pricing.

[13] See, for example, A. Kneese and C. Schultze, *Pollution, Prices, and Public Policy* (Washington, D.C., Brookings Institution, 1975).

[14] The EPA has commissioned a consultant's report on the land use impact of federal interceptor sewer subsidies. The findings so far have produced perhaps the best data base presently available for consideration of this problem. See Urban Systems Research and Engineering, Inc., "Interceptor Sewers and Suburban Sprawl," draft final report (July 31, 1974).

[15] See W. R. Hughes, "Sale Frontiers in Electric Power," in W. Capron, ed., *Technological Change in Regulated Industries* (Washington, D.C., Brookings Institution, 1971).

Finally, there is the investment planning problem. Characteristic of all of the public utility services, it arises from the inherent characteristics of the technologies and is exacerbated by some of the institutional arrangements for planning and delivering these services. Water and sewerage capacity requirements have generally been based upon projections of need—that is, physical definitions of future consumption—derived from current per capita use figures and projections of expected population growth, the latter being derived from extrapolations of past growth. But population growth is only one factor determining future service demand, and it is questionable that it is the best available indicator for timing and sizing of capacity expansion. On the contrary, there is considerable evidence that it is not, and that extrapolations based upon growth trends result in undependable capacity requirement forecasts.

Table 4-2 identifies the major distortions in water and sewerage service pricing and investment policy.

Electricity

Table 4-1, which identifies the comparable phases of three urban public utility services, describes the cost structure of electricity production and distribution in a metropolitan area. Characteristically, electricity is generated at several plant sites in and around a metropolitan area. Some of the electricity consumed in that area originates as "bulk power," that is, power purchased at wholesale rates under interchange or pooling agreements with other electric utilities outside the metropolitan area. Undoubtedly, there are internal economies of scale in electricity generation for plants that generate up to 1,000 MWe (megawatts electric); but whether economies of scale extend beyond this point is not clear.[16] This means that, up to 1,000 MWe, larger base load generating plants are cheaper per kilowatt hour generated at the plant bus bar (the terminal at which plant power lines join external transmission lines). The distinction between bus bar power and delivered power is important. There has been a tendency to invoke economies of scale as a justification for particular rate structures,[17] and to overlook the simple economic

[16] See, for example, W. Vennard, *The Electric Power Business* (2 ed., New York, McGraw-Hill, 1970).

[17] Utilities are highly sophisticated cost-minimizers in this sense; and where cost has been defined to include external costs that more-inclusive cost is effectively minimized. For example, in the Southern California Edison service area an implicit price on air emissions is imposed in the form of air quality standards at certain times, and generating units are fired in inverse emission order.

TABLE 4-2. Public Utility Service Pricing and Investment "Distortions"

Service	Cost allocation and pricing	Investment
Water and sewerage	Allocation of capacity costs between special and normal users.	Price-independent capacity requirement projections
	Spatially undifferentiated rates.	Capacity requirement projections based upon extrapolation of population growth trends
	Capacity charges based upon noncoincident demand.	and high gallon-day estimates
		Failure to charge new users incremental costs of services
		Federal wastewater treatment and interceptor sewer construction grants
Electricity	Spatially undifferentiated rates; minimum bill does not properly register identifiable customer costs.	Price-independent capacity requirement projections
		Capacity requirement projections based upon growth-trended system at peak demand
	Temporally undifferentiated rates; declining-block demand charges based upon noncoincident demand.	
	Calculation of capital costs (as allowed return on original cost) underprices incremental capacity costs.	
Intraurban transportation	Social costs (pollution, congestion) unpriced.	Price-independent capacity projections
	Motor fuel excises and motor vehicle fees underprice peak-hour limited-access highway capacity.	Capacity projections for limited access highway based upon growth-trended "need"

fact that, at a given moment, all electricity users are "marginal" customers, coequally responsible for the incurrence of capacity costs and also coequally entitled to the benefits of lower electricity prices of whatever scale economies their aggregate consumption may allow. Further, though there are plant economies of scale, up to 1,000 MWe, in a long-term sense, at any given moment, system generation is characterized by short-term increasing costs, since the plants are of varying ages and efficiencies and capital operating cost characteristics, and because the plants are fired in increasing variable cost order.[18] Again, there is no simple line of argument from long-term decreasing generation costs to our present declining-block rate structures.

Generating costs are usually thought to be from one-third to one-half the cost of delivered residential power: for example, estimates range from 10 mills for power generation and 20 mills for its delivery. But such a comparison of costs is potentially misleading, for it is important to distinguish between the cost of generating power at the system's peak and off-peak hours. Peak-hour customers are disproportionately responsible for increased generating capacity costs that often reach as much as half of total system capacity costs. Depending upon the method used in allocating capacity costs between peak-hour and off-peak users, estimates of peak-hour generation costs can be as high as 50 mills and those for off-peak generation as low as zero mills—figures that differ substantially from the above-average cost estimate. Transmission and distribution system losses are calculable and assignable to individual customers. These losses are not traditionally included in the definitions of transmission and distribution costs.

Still, generating capacity costs are only a part of total system capacity costs. Electricity must be transmitted to distribution system substations, from substations to distribution lines, and from distribution lines to the users, with numerous voltage reductions—requiring investment in transformers—occurring along the way. The lowest voltages are generally delivered to residential customers, with larger commercial and industrial customers accepting higher-voltage power. This does not mean that a customer requiring less power is cheaper to serve than a larger user, although often this will be the case. Because of distribution cost differentials, customers closer to the power plant may be cheaper to serve than more-distant smaller users.

Given the diversity of customer locations and the spatial network that transmission and distribution systems must occupy, the long-run cost characteristics of transmission and distribution systems are relatively simple. Because physically larger systems allow transmission and distribution at higher voltages—resulting in lower power losses—long-run decreasing costs in transmission and distribution are possible. However,

[18] See, for example, M. F. Sharefkin, *The Economic and Environmental Benefits from Improving Electrical Rate Structures,* EPA-600/5-74-033 (Washington, D.C., Govt. Print. Off., November 1974).

that cost structure does not mean lower kilowatt-hour prices for larger
users: causal responsibility for the incurrence of system transmission
and distribution costs is better reflected in rate structures in the form of
lump sum charges, which are assessed independently of total consumption.

The allocation among individual users of the distribution system's
capital costs presents problems similar in principle to the allocation of
the generation plant's capital cost. They each have a joint cost or peak-
load problem: working backward along the physical linkage from consumption point to generation point, the problem becomes more serious.
That linkage requires a drop line from the distribution line to the user's
dwelling, a common distribution line to the distribution substation, and
subtransmission and transmission lines to the generating plant bus bar.
The costs for the drop line serving a single customer are unambiguously
imposed by, and assignable to, that user. But, as we move back along
the linkage between customer and generating station, the capital cost is
harder to assign. Distribution and transmission line capacity costs are
incurred jointly in the service of all customers using that capacity at
peak,[19] so that these costs should be assigned to peak-period customers.
Again, and this is the hallmark of the joint cost problem, these costs
cannot be correctly allocated in ignorance of demand conditions. Thus,
cost allocation shades into pricing.

Pricing of electricity.   A regulatory determination of electricity rates
typically follows the same sequence as that noted for other utilities.
First, the revenue requirement is determined. Next, the rate structure is
set. As with water and sewerage rates, there is enormous diversity in
the tariffs used by U.S. electric utilities, as is apparent from a glance at
the Federal Power Commission's (FPC's) compilation of U.S. electricity
rates.[20]

There is no nationally circulated "consensus" handbook on electricity
rate practices comparable to the Water Rates Manual; the formal work
of the Edison Electric Institute's rate committee is the closest approxi-
mation. Nevertheless, a kind of national practice does exist, drawing its

[19] Federal Power Commission, *National Electric Rate Book* (Washington, D.C.,
Govt. Print. Off., 1974).
[20] For an account of the origins and rationale of American electricity tariff
practices, see Kahn, *The Economics of Regulation,* vol. I.

theoretical underpinnings from traditional public utility cost-allocation procedures. These common elements of national practice, rather than the rate practice of any particular system, will be our focus here.

Almost all U.S. electric utilities classify their customers as residential, commercial, or industrial (that is, large power users). Residential costs are nearly all based on declining block rates: under this rate formula a customer's monthly bill depends only upon his own total consumption and is computed by weighting successive discrete consumption intervals by successively lower per-kilowatt-hour prices. Therefore, the marginal price is lower than the average price.

It is often claimed that declining block rates are cost-justified, which assumes that each customer's usage imposes upon the system costs which "can be decomposed" into customer costs, capacity costs, and energy (commodity) costs. Traditionally, these costs are defined as follows: *customer costs* are those costs—such as metering, billing, and some general and administrative costs—which depend only upon the total number of customers in the system; *capacity costs* are those costs which depend only upon total (coincident or noncoincident) system maximum demand; and *energy costs* are those costs which depend only upon total consumption.[21]

The argument for declining block rates proceeds as follows from this cost classification: first, customer costs are allocated among customer classes, and then among subcategories within each customer class. Those allocated amounts are the minimum cost for each customer class, that is, the amount each customer must pay to be connected to the system, even at zero consumption. Next, rate block heights and kilowatt-hour lengths must be defined. For our purpose, suppose that there are two blocks. The second block, or "tailblock," is the one at which all electricity consumption greater than some specific kilowatt-hour total is billed, and the first block extends from zero consumption to that kilowatt-hour total. The two remaining functional cost components—capacity costs and energy costs—must be recovered from the customer under these two blocks. If the tailblock height is equal to the energy charge, then the capacity costs imposed by the user must be entirely recovered in the first block; thus, we get a declining block-rate structure. In practice, the

---

[21] This statement overlooks many subtleties: the variable costs of producing an incremental kilowatt-hour vary enormously, typically from 7 mills for base load power to 20 mills or more for gas turbine peaking power.

height of the tailblock is generally somewhat higher than the average operating and maintenance costs incurred in producing a kilowatt-hour of electricity,[22] so that, under declining block tariffs, capacity costs are being recovered from both the intermediate blocks (in our two-block illustration, it is the first block alone) and the tailblock.

Two features of declining block-rate pricing—applicable to almost all U.S. residential and small commercial users[23]—are especially important. The use of a noncoincident peak measure of causal responsibility for imposed capacity cost blurs the assignment of capacity costs; and the declining block rate means that customers face marginal prices that are lower than average prices. The time-honored argument for declining block residential and small commercial rates—that larger users are "more responsible" for the economies of scale that the system can exploit, and, therefore, they deserve to be rewarded with quantity discounts—is fallacious. If there are economies of scale in the provision of some service, then efficiency requires that all users be charged the lower per unit price allowed by such economies—with no quantity discounts. It is argued that equitable recovery of the capital costs requires that larger users be charged lower per kilowatt-hour distribution costs. But identifiable distribution costs should be assessed as components of the minimum bill— as lump sum charges, independent of consumption—and not spread over consumption.

Electricity sold to large commercial and industrial users is usually priced through a minimum bill and two declining block rate structures. Customer costs are recovered in a minimum bill; capacity costs are recovered through a declining block rate structure applied to the customer's maximum noncoincident kilowatt demand, that is, the customer's maximum demand, whenever it occurs. A second declining block rate structure is then used to compute a charge based upon the customer's total monthly kilowatt-hour consumption. The customer's total monthly bill is then the sum of the minimum bill and the charges computed under the two declining block rate structures. Thus, the two major problems

[22] Again, some distinctions are blurred here. Many systems have interruptible power as a rate option; some systems charge some part of industrial user capacity costs as coincident peak charges, thus shading into a kind of peak-load pricing.

[23] To my knowledge, there is no comprehensive U.S. survey of electric utility load forecasting practices; a partial study is that of the Federal Power Commission, *The 1970 National Power Survey* (Washington, D.C., Govt. Print. Off., 1970).

of the residential block rate structure also plague large commercial and industrial electricity rate schedules; the billing of capacity charges on a noncoincident demand basis is especially important. Peak-hour customers disproportionately impose capacity costs on the system and should therefore be billed on a maximum coincident demand basis.

Investment in the electricity plant.   U.S. electric utilities have based their capacity requirements on projections of growth in the system's peak demand but generally have not figured prices into these forecasts. Though electric utilities differ considerably in the practice of load forecasting,[24] available summaries of best-practice support this generalization.

There is an extremely simple method for forecasting peak demand: the system peak for the past several years is used as a basis for the trend growth rate. The future peak demand is then forecast for the planning period of the system—generally eight to ten years, the characteristic lead time required from plant design and siting approval to operation—by adding the peak demand trend to the reserve capacity margin. That margin is the capacity required, over and above peak demand, in order to ensure that peak demand will be met. The rules of thumb employed, separately or in conjunction, are (1) that total capacity be 20 percent greater than system peak demand; (2) that there be, at any given time, enough reserve capacity to meet system demand in the event of the failure of the largest generating unit running; or (3) that the probability of a failure to meet load requirements be the equivalent of one brownout- or blackout-day in ten years.

During a period of relatively stable growth, even if that growth is relatively rapid, rules like this can be fairly accurate. But in a period of relatively unstable load growth—associated with changes in relative prices, changes in the rate of growth of demand, or both—capacity-expansion rules of this kind may be seriously misleading. Forecasting

[24] For a sense of how widely long-term energy demand forecasts differ, compare D. Chapman, G. C. Akland, J. Finklea et al., "Power Generation: Conservation, Health and Fuel Supply," report to the Task Force on Conservation and Fuel Supply, Technical Advisory Committee on Conservation of Energy, with, for example, electric utility industry expansion plans, as summarized by the nine regional national electric reliability councils. The councils report consistent 8 percent annual growth rates over the period 1973–80; the demand analyses of Chapman et al. indicate growth rates of less than 4 percent over these same years.

capacity requirements in a period of unstable growth is genuinely difficult;[25] as is noted below, adherence to dated rules of thumb may be as much the result of perverse incentives as of intrinsic uncertainty.

The aberrant features of the capacity planning process can be seen in table 4-2.

Transportation

Transportation is traditionally considered one of the public utility services: traditional, dating from the turn of the century, European rail-pricing debates are one source of our present utility-pricing theory, and the first major American experiment in regulatory administration, the Interstate Commerce Commission (ICC), was initially a rail-oriented agency.

Of the three public utility services, transportation is most central to the determination of patterns of intraurban settlement. Changes in transportation technologies and in the costs of transportation services have been the key determinant of the rate of urban decentralization. Distortions in the pricing of transportation services are therefore probably more serious than distortions in the pricing and investment strategies of the other services, since the former impose larger efficiency losses. It might seem that the opportunities for improvement are similarly larger here, but the transportation sector is complicated in ways that the other public utilities are not, and it is important to be mindful of those differences. First, intraurban transportation is not regulated by a single public authority nor managed by one publicly regulated firm. Both the "public" subsector—intraurban bus or rail rapid transit[26]—and the "private" subsector—interurban automobile and truck traffic—are heavily public. The first is public in the more conventional sense of public ownership or public regulation of metropolitan bus facilities. For example, the number of buses, the allocation of bus routes and the scheduling of runs, the level and structure of fares, and the size of the subsidy to finance an operating deficit, if any, are matters of public decision. The second

[25] For a discussion of the long-term trend toward decentralization of urban areas and of the role of changing relative transportation prices in that trend, see E. Mills, *Studies in the Structure of the Urban Economy* (Baltimore, Johns Hopkins University Press for Resources for the Future, 1972).

[26] Our emphasis here is upon public interurban bus and private automobile and truck transportation; few American cities are likely to build rail rapid transit systems, in part because of the San Franscico Bay Area Rapid Transit experience.

is public in a somewhat different sense: there are significant public inputs into the production of all intraurban transportation services. The automobile commuter or shopper combines privately purchased inputs with the capital service flows of the publicly provided right-of-way—and with other publicly provided inputs, such as traffic control and violations enforcement—to produce transportation services.

This mix of private and public provision, and the role of the consumer as a producer in the private sector, are two of the significant complications associated with transportation policy. The first problem bedevils empirical work on the urban transportation cost structures. For example, historic data on the acquisition cost of right-of-way may have little relationship to the opportunity costs of withdrawal of that land from the private sector. And the second problem plagues cost–benefit analyses of proposed transportation improvements, since measures of the value of commuter time saved are somewhat arbitrary. More troublesome than either of these problems, perhaps, is the range of "commodities" traded in intraurban transportation service markets. For example, trips between distinct pairs of origin destination points at different times of the day are essentially different commodities. The electric utilities share this problem, but there it is made easier by orders of magnitude: it is relatively easy to define homogeneous classes of electricity consumers.

For intraurban automobile trips, cost structures are extremely complex because most trips exploit both unlimited access, or "local" roads, and limited access roads or freeways. The administrative costs of appropriately pricing both parts of each trip are generally cited as the major impediment to pricing reform of intraurban transportation. The probable distribution of gains and losses from changes in the pricing—and institutional constraints on the shifting of those gains and losses—are perhaps the more reasonable explanation.

The cost structure of intraurban bus transportation is considerably simpler to describe, and the design of efficient pricing schemes for intraurban bus service is correspondingly easier in principle, though there may be important institutional barriers to such implementation. Consequently, one of the more persuasive arguments for increased reliance on public transportation, suggests that publicly operated intraurban transportation can, in principle, be efficiently priced, so that social benefits of efficient patterns of intraurban location can be realized only with a largely public intraurban transportation system.

So much for the difficulties in precisely explaining intraurban transportation cost structures: the characteristic distortions are impressive enough that even a rough knowledge of cost structure is a useful benchmark.

The public inputs into intraurban automobile transport include the capital, operating, and maintenance costs of local unlimited access automobile right-of-way and limited access (or freeway) right-of-way. These costs are, in the aggregate, relatively easy to estimate (their proper allocation between users—pricing—and their present incidence are a very different matter). More elusive and controversial are the social costs of intraurban automobile traffic—congestion and air and noise pollution. Congestion costs are imposed upon all concurrent users of a right-of-way by all other users: when access to a right-of-way is unrestricted, that right-of-way will be inefficiently overutilized. This problem has been long recognized; the reluctance of governments, transportation authorities, and commuters to grasp the economist's proposed solution—congestion charges—indicates more than stubbornness. The pollution costs of automobile traffic in cities are almost entirely air pollution costs. Though the automobile is but one source of air pollution in metropolitan areas, it is a major source, important enough in some areas to be a problem even in the absence of stationary sources of air pollutants. Again, these costs are difficult to quantify;[27] nevertheless, the governance of air quality in metropolitan areas is necessarily bound up with the regulation of automobile traffic. Under the 1970 amendments to the Clean Air Act, all states are required to file implementation plans, one component of which is a comprehensive transportation plan for SMSAs within each state's boundaries.[28]

As noted above, intraurban automobile trips between different points, and at different times of the day, are really different goods. But for our purposes, it is sufficient to divide the day into two distinct time periods: the peak (or rush) hours of commuting between workplaces and residences, and the off-peak hours, in which most trips are not to and from

[27] See, for example, the relevant portions of L. B. Barrett and T. E. Waddell, *The Cost of Air Pollution Damages,* Publication Number AP-85 (Research Triangle Park, N.C., EPA, February 1973).

[28] For a caustic analysis and critique of the implementation plan process see the testimony of R. Ayres in *Implementation of the Clean Air Act Amendments,* Hearing before the Senate Subcommittee on Air and Water Pollution, 92 Cong. 2 sess. (1972).

workplaces. The capacity costs of right-of-way are disproportionately the causal responsibility of peak-hour commuters: this has important implications when present transportation pricing schemes are measured against an efficiency standard under which consumers of transportation pay the full incremental costs that they impose.

The cost structure for intraurban bus transportation is similar, except for one obvious and essential difference, to that for interurban automobile transportation. It is not clear, even in principle, how passenger time should be valued: a full opportunity cost measure may not be appropriate, since the time is not useless. But this problem is less serious than it is for automobile transportation, since the major variable inputs to intraurban bus transportation are the fuel and the operator's labor— and these costs are directly incurred, as pecuniary costs, by the transportation authority.

Pricing of intrametropolitan transportation.   The special features of intrametropolitan transportation have generated procedures and conventions for allocating costs to users, which have, in turn, given us price structures that many economists regard as a major source of resource misallocation in urban areas.[29] Beginning with private automobile transport, the variable inputs supplied by the individual commuter—his or her own scarce time and the operating and maintenance costs of the automobile—are either priced on an imputed basis or priced explicitly in markets. Pollution and congestion aside, costs and prices are relatively similar for these inputs.

The serious cost–price distortions are associated with the publicly provided inputs, especially the land and capital required to provide right-of-way. The provision and maintenance of right-of-way takes place under an enormous variety of financial and institutional arrangements.[30] Consider, first, the arrangements under which federal, state, and local governments share in the capital costs of roads, arrangements specified

[29] See, for example, E. Mills, "Markets and Efficient Resource Allocation in Urban Areas," *Swedish Journal of Economics* vol. 74, no. 1 (March 1972); and A. A. Walters, *The Economics of Road User Charges* (Baltimore, Johns Hopkins University Press, 1968).

[30] For fairly obvious reasons, roads other than exclusively local roads must be financed, in part, by higher units of government, since—if road access is unpriced—they provide spillover benefits to residents of other jurisdictions. But the arrangements under which interjurisdictional transfers for road construction have been made have little to do with this kind of "optimal federalism."

in the authorizing legislation under which the interstate system and the federally aided state systems have been built. Federal law specifies only the state shares of total land acquisition and road construction costs and grants the state governments broad latitude in choosing revenue sources. The financing arrangements devised by the states are predictably diverse, as a glance at the essential provisions of these arrangements makes clear.[31] But both state highways and state shares of state–federal highways are funded, wholly or in large measure, from state motor vehicle fuel taxes and vehicle registration fees. Similarly, the federal highway trust fund, the endowment which finances the federal share of joint state–federal highway construction, is built upon federal motor vehicle fuel excises. The intent of these financing arrangements is obviously that the beneficiaries of the service flows provided by these investments—in this case, the highway users—pay the costs of providing those service flows.

The problem with using gasoline excise taxes to price highway access— a problem long suspected to be important in principle, but one which has frustrated efforts at definitive quantification[32]—is that this is a very clumsy way of pricing highway capacity. The situation recalls the electricity pricing problem, where present off-peak prices are too high, needlessly discouraging off-peak consumption, and peak-hour prices are too low, forcing the installation of an inefficiently large generating capacity. In the case of highways, the "average-cost" gasoline excise-tax pricing of highway access underprices the peak commuting hours and overprices the services of urban highways at off-peak hours and the services of rural highways at all hours. Cost estimates have tended to confirm this: The classic study of Meyer, Kain, and Wohl[33] went further, indicating that there were substantial efficiency gains realizable through price rationing of freeway access, and later work has confirmed these conclusions.[34]

[31] See U.S. Department of Transportation and Federal Highway Administration, *Highway Statistics 1971* (Washington, D.C., Govt. Print. Off., 1971) pp. 12–29.

[32] I have been unable to find any empirical estimate of welfare loss from the gasoline-tax mispricing of American highways. H. Mohring, in a related theoretical article ["The Peak Load Problem with Increasing Returns and Pricing Constraints," *American Economic Review* vol. 60, no. 4 (September 1970), p. 693] cites work in progress on this question.

[33] J. Meyer, J. Kain, and M. Wohl, *The Urban Transportation Problem* (Cambridge, Mass., Harvard University Press, 1965).

[34] See, for example, A. A. Walters, *The Economics of Road User Charges* (Baltimore, Johns Hopkins University Press, 1968).

An alternative, second-best approach to estimating the efficiency losses imposed by the mispricing of urban peak-hour highway capacity begins with the assumption that the gasoline tax is the sole feasible instrument for pricing of urban highways and streets, and then calculates the optimum tax, given that this tax must establish the optimum level of congestion. Calculations done more than ten years ago put this tax at around fifty cents per gallon—much higher than current gasoline taxes[35]—and higher than today's gasoline "conservation" tax proposals.

Turning to the pricing of urban bus transit, there is no national rate-making handbook nor any consistent national pattern upon which to base an analysis of pricing practices. Here, as in the cases of other public utility services, the practices of different metropolitan areas vary considerably. But two kinds of pricing systems are sufficiently popular to warrant citation and discussion here. In the first, a single-fare system, where one fixed payment buys admission to the system at any point and at any time at which the system is operating, the passenger is free to ride anywhere in the system or anywhere within the portion of the system linked by original route and transfers to the point of entry. In the second, a system of spatially differentiated fares, payment is for transit between a specific origin and a specific destination, and the structure of fares is calculated on a per-mile basis. Even if fares are the same for each route, there are route distance bins and different fares for each bin.[36]

Neither of these pricing schemes does a particularly good job of matching up cost and price. The cost structure of urban bus service is such that per-mile operating costs (essentially, the driver's salary and the operating and maintenance costs of the bus) are roughly the same for all operating hours,[37] so that time-undifferentiated rates set to recover per-mile operating costs imply a cross subsidy from peak to off-peak

[35] A. A. Walters, "The Theory and Measurement of Private and Social Cost of Highway Congestion," *Econometrica* vol. 29, no. 4 (October 1961).

[36] The staffs of several metropolitan area transportation authorities have written uncirculated studies of time-differentiated fare schemes, but to the best of my knowledge, only the Washington Metropolitan Transport Authority has implemented such a fare scheme. Several widely used devices—such as reduced fares to senior citizens in off-peak hours—are steps toward peak-load pricing; of course, these devices have income distributional as well as efficiency objectives.

[37] A significant cost component of the total social cost of bus operation—passenger time—is not discussed here at all, largely because it is not essential to either the optimization of bus service or to the setting of fares. Indeed, other transport cost components are more important in this respect.

users. For our present purposes, note that this pricing scheme restricts peak-hour use of urban bus transportation and encourages peak-hour auto commutation. The question of how much remains unsettled, but econometric evidence suggests that cross-price elasticities between intra-urban transportation modes are relatively small,[38] and that the cross-price elasticities of changes in service quality—in particular, changes in waiting time—are much larger. In any event, those econometric estimates are based upon data for a period over which price variations were much smaller than the differences between present and "efficient" peak-hour prices. If we take seriously econometric estimates of the under-pricing of auto-imposed congestion,[39] and imagine that correct congestion charges could be imposed upon all vehicle transport, the increase in auto transport prices would be substantially larger than the previous range of price variation upon which the econometric estimates have been based. The implication is that we have underestimated the intermodal elasticity of substitution.

For reasons that are largely apparent, congestion pricing proposals for urban streets have seldom been taken seriously. Given that auto congestion of urban streets cannot be priced, the second-best proposal has been that bus transport be subsidized by covering operating deficits out of general revenues. Alternatively, it has been suggested that bus transport be implicitly subsidized by the preferential allocation of scarce peak-hour freeway capacity to buses; the so-called exclusive bus lanes, sometimes modified as exclusive lanes for buses and fully occupied cars. These schemes seem to us to be desirable first steps toward an improved urban transportation system.

Investment in intrametropolitan transport capacity. The highway investment process—for both interstate and federally aided state systems and the system of state highways—is somewhat similar to the process of capacity expansion in water and sewerage. But the disparities, arising from the differentiating features of the transportation sector, are equally striking. As in the case of capacity planning for other public utility services, there are long lead times from inception to completion of highway projects. For example, planning, land acquisition, and con-

[38] For a summary, see G. Kraft, "Free Transit Revisited," *Public Policy* vol. 20, no. 1 (Winter 1972).
[39] Walters, "The Theory and Measurement."

struction can take up to eight years. Again, capacity requirements have generally been forecast on a "need" basis, with need being calculated by extrapolating present traffic flows—on the basis of past growth trends or on gravity models of trip generation, that is, models based upon populations at specified origins and definitions. Neither method incorporates economic measures of "required" capacity. These pricing and investment policy distortions for transportation have been summarized in table 4-2.

THE GOVERNANCE OF PUBLIC UTILITIES

Explanations of Persistent Distortions

The derivation of normative pricing and investment rules for the public utility services is one of the oldest preoccupations of quantitative economics; for example, Dupuit's seminal contribution dates from 1844.[40] Still, the influence of this work on the pricing and investment practices of U.S. public utilities has been almost negligible.

Popular explanations of this aspect of regulatory failure are typically couched in institutional terms and cover a broad range of possibilities. There are supply-oriented arguments, built upon assumptions about the organizational objectives of the public utility managers and public service commissions. There are also demand-oriented arguments based upon assumptions about the incentives and opportunities for collective action among consumers of these services.

The hallmark of these kinds of explanations is their descriptive realism. But they have not been developed into an explicit positive theory of pricing and investment behavior. And rarely are they incorporated into normative approaches to public utility regulation, a necessary first step in the reform of the public utility regulatory bodies.

In order to strike out in that direction, we must first distinguish between supply- and demand-oriented arguments.

The Objectives of Regulated Firms and Regulatory Commissions

The supply-oriented explanation of regulatory failure is as follows: some critics claim that insufficiently expert utility and commission personnel

[40] J. Dupuit, "On the Measurement of the Utility of Public Works," as reprinted in K. Arrow and T. Scitovsky, eds., Readings in Welfare Economics (Homewood, Ill., Richard D. Irwin, 1969).

are incapable of understanding the arguments for reform of rate and planning systems. However appealing this explanation may be to long-time participants in regulatory proceedings, there is no reason for stating that personnel incompetence produces a universal predilection for declining-block rates in electricity pricing, biases toward excess highway capacity, systematic overbuilding of interceptor sewerage capacity, or for anything else.

Others argue that reforming the present rate structures to cover administrative and transaction costs would result in even higher prices. In some situations this argument is clearly right; for example, in a strict sense every electricity user imposes different costs upon society, but the administrative costs of billing every customer on his own rate schedule are prohibitive. However, this argument is frequently invoked in situations where it is almost certainly mistaken, for example, in discussions of peak-load pricing for electricity and transportation systems.

It is pointed out by still others that regulatory agencies and the utilities they regulate have goals other than those specified in their charters. And, because of this, they are reluctant to advocate various reform proposals. Of all the explanations for regulatory failure, this last one seems most appropriate.

Models of this kind can be helpful in identifying the institutional causes of the problems plaguing public utility service delivery, and they can point the way toward a normative theory of public utility service governance. The literature on the utilities and their regulatory commissions offers some objectives to explore in our efforts to explain pricing and investment patterns. Elements of some, or all, of the following commission models are intermingled, and each such stereotypical commission embodies some definite assumption about the objectives of the regulatory commission or regulated firm or authority.[41]

The conflict-of-interest commission. The individual commission members seek, through their leverage over the timing and siting of investment, to maximize the value of landholdings of their own, or the value of landholdings of others whom they represent on the regulatory commission.

[41] For a review of the somewhat more traditional theories of regulation see R. A. Posner, "Theories of Economic Regulation," *Bell Journal of Economics and Management Science* vol. 5, no. 2 (Autumn 1974) p. 335.

The growth-oriented commission or regulated firm. The objectives of the commission or firm are not the traditional regulatory objectives—such as revenue maximization subject to rate-of-return constraint—but rather the kind of objectives characteristically assumed in much recent work on the theory of the firm, that is, either sales or growth maximization.[42]

The shuttlecock commission. The regulatory commission, and, at times, both it and the regulated firm, are passive equilibrators of the conflicting pressures exerted by groups organized around, or organized by, the regulatory process. Those groups include the individual customer classes, the usual consumer interest groups, producer groups, and, more recently, environmental groups. The commission's actions are the result of a least-resistance response to pressure.[43]

We need not select one of these models over the other two. What we want are helpful lines of inquiry into the distortions of rate making and investment policy which we have identified above. Under this criterion, the last two models have their uses, but the first can be disregarded. That first model is difficult to validate, though there is abundant supportive anecdotal evidence, especially in case studies of water utilities.

The shuttlecock commission model can, in its extreme form, become too spongy, explaining almost anything as the outcome of pressure group action. Still, it has its uses, and it will be invoked in what follows.

Passive Customer Classes Versus Active Coalitions

In most analyses of public utility pricing and investment the different customer classes are treated as essentially homogeneous in their load and other characteristics and as having distinct demand functions. Once these demand functions have been determined, normative pricing and investment rules are established. In principle, this framework can be extended to include analysis of the optimum customer classification, with the administrative and informational costs of finer customer clas-

---

[42] For a review of the literature, see J. Williamson, "Profit, Growth and Sales Maximization," *Economica* vol. 33, no. 129 (February 1966).

[43] Along these lines, an intriguing look at the process of electric utility rate regulation can be found in P. Joskow, "Inflation and Environmental Concern: Structural Change in the Process of Public Utility Price Regulation," MIT Department of Economics Working Paper Number 128 (March 1974).

sification balanced against the benefits associated with an improved matching of prices and costs. Thus, there is an obvious hypothesis regarding the variation in customer classification and rate structural detail observed across samples of public utility systems: these systems classify customers, and design rates, on efficiency grounds.

How much explanatory power will this hypothesis have? My strong impression is that the answer is, not much. There often seems to be little correlation between the tariff type and the obvious variables—system size, number of customers, and so on—so that formulation and testing of alternative theories of customer classification and, more generally, of collective action by consumers of public utility services, seems warranted. A difficult and novel feature of utility pricing problems is the leverage which suppliers, by choosing certain rate structures, customer classifications, and spatial patterns of rate differentiation, can exert over the possibilities for collective action. There can be significant nonprice interdependence of demand and supply sides.

Nevertheless, I will begin by identifying what might be called the natural demand-oriented coalitions. A reasonable assumption is that these coalitions organize with the expectation that costs incurred by coalition members will buy favorable price and service area decisions by the regulatory agency. The costs incurred include those of forming the coalition and the legal and other costs of intervention in rate cases and representation before regulatory commissions. Typically, organizing costs can be expected to increase with the number of customers to be organized and with their spatial dispersion. The so-called natural coalitions—those with relatively low organization costs—can be identified, and some guesses can be made as to which public utilities these coalitions will most likely influence.

1. Locational coalitions can be described as suburban ring and inner core coalitions. Since the suburban ring and urban core are generally distinct political entities, the machinery is in place for coalition formation along jurisdictional or locational lines, and where the regulatory jurisdictions are similarly patterned the impulse will be that much stronger. If ring jurisdictions are affluent, with high per capita consumption of the public utility service, decisive pressure for rate structures favoring these jurisdictions can be anticipated.

2. Old and new coalitions might be described, respectively, as coalitions of new users and of existing users. To the extent that there are high costs incurred in the development of new residential areas, new development is already organized to exert pressure on regulated firms and regulatory commissions. Any one customer class is a potential coalition, since—barring redefinition of customer classes—it faces the same rate structure. Again, customer classes consisting of fewer numbers of larger users will have lower organization costs, and lower barriers to coalition formation, than customer classes of higher numbers of smaller users.

3. The possibility exists for the formation of coalitions of predominantly off-peak and predominantly peak users. This is more probable when other obvious correlates of load factor exist, such as customer size.

4. And, finally, there are what might be called environmental cost coalitions. These are coalitions of customers and noncustomers whose primary concern is with the external costs of the public utilities—though these external costs may, in some cases, be disproportionately incurred by individuals who are not consumers of the particular public utility.

These coalitions exist in one form or another; for example, ring versus core coalitions in transportation, old versus new coalitions in water and sewerage, customer class coalitions in electricity pricing, and environmental cost coalitions in all of these services. How are the relative pressures these coalitions can bring to bear on the regulatory process governed by the rules under which that process operated? How will changes in these rules affect the outcome of this process? What are criteria for a "good" regulatory process?

Effect of Regulation on Pricing

We have repeatedly emphasized, in our discussions of the individual public utilities, the centrality of the joint cost problem. A major portion of public utility costs are jointly incurred. Though there is a way to allocate these joint costs efficiently, when the demands of identifiable customer classes are known unambiguously, the individual customer class demand functions are often unknown, so that these joint costs cannot be "properly" allocated.

Ignorance of demand conditions, contrived or necessary, makes for considerable discretion in the allocation of joint costs. Either the growth-oriented commission model, or the shuttlecock commission model then generates a predictive theory of joint cost allocation, and hence a derived predictive theory of rate structure design.[44]

But, even where cost allocations are imposed upon regulated firms, there is some room for price maneuvering—so long as some prices can depart from cost. Definitionally, the sales or growth-oriented commission will set prices in order to maximize sales or the rate of growth sales, respectively. This will require price discrimination in favor of relatively elastic users at the expense of relatively inelastic users. Assuming a profit constraint—either zero economic profit or some specified rate of return on rate base—costs can be recovered by recovering more than incremental costs from inelastic users. The shuttlecock commission will price somewhat differently, recovering joint costs from customer classes in inverse proportion to the pressures those customer classes, or their organized interest groups, can bring to bear on the rate-making process.

Can we see traces of these objectives in present rate patterns? Consider the "time-related" distortions in the pricing of all of the metropolitan public utilities, which we have listed previously: the failure to recover full costs from peak users in the case of electricity and water, and the inverse failure—cross subsidization of off-peak users by peak-hour users—in the case of urban bus transport. For growth-oriented water and electricity commissions or firms, the policy makes sense, depending upon the own-price and cross-price elasticities of service demand on peak-hour and off-peak consumption. Here, again, the implication is that underpricing of the peak-hour consumption is compatible with sales maximization.

Turning from time-related to spatial pricing distortions, consider the problem which the sales or growth-maximizing commission faces in recovering the costs of the utility's physical distribution system. Given the flexibility they have in cost allocation, the sales or growth-maximizing firm or commission will exploit spatially correlated demand patterns. Thus, if price elasticities of demand are higher in the suburban ring than in the core, allocations of the distribution system costs will favor the

[44] The cost allocation may or may not be explicit, and may or may not become public. Commissions vary widely in what information they require in support of a rate request; some require a cost of service study while others do not. I know of no comparative study for the public utility service commissions.

suburban ring at the expense of the core. The firm or commission will be reluctant to correctly price the distribution capacity.

It is likely that this happens in the provision of two of the public utilities—water and sewerage and electricity.[45] The opportunities to distort prices in this direction are several. Minimum bills, which should reflect at least those costs for which the individual customer bears sole responsibility, are often uniform over an entire metropolitan area; in the Washington, D.C., SMSA, where regulatory commission governance is split between several regulatory commissions, minimum bills typically do not even capture interjurisdictional differentials in average distribution cost. But there is an even clearer indication of this tendency: the failure of many electric utilities to charge for the long individual house distribution lines often required to service fringe area development.[46]

In summary, a good deal of the available evidence on the pricing of the public utility services is compatible with sales or growth-maximizing behavior. But it is difficult to conclude that this explanation should be adopted over other equally plausible ones. Thus, for example, an electric utility which is subject to rate base regulation will be inefficiently capital-intensive in a way made familiar to us by Averch and Johnson.[47] According to Averch and Johnson, a firm subject to a peak-load problem will necessarily distort prices in a way that favors peak-hour users over off-peak users. I do not regard this particular example as especially serious; there is wide skepticism as to the empirical relevance of the Averch-Johnson effect.[48] In any event, I am tempted to argue that we are unlikely to be able to discriminate between different behavioral models of regulated firms and regulatory commissions with the data that we have now; and that we are unlikely to get significantly better data short of institutional changes in the governance of the public utilities.

[45] See, for the case of water and sewerage, P. Downing, "Extension of Sewer Service at the Urban Fringe," *Land Economics* vol. 45, no. 1 (February 1969) p. 103. For electricity, empirical work of my own, in progress at RFF, leans in this direction; the arguments in the text of this paper, built on general cost allocation procedures, are probably the strongest that can be made here.

[46] In the Washington, D.C., area, the rule has been up to 100 feet of line free. Since suburban Montgomery County requires the undergrounding of all distribution lines this can amount to $1,000 in installed costs; minimum bills of less than $2 per month do not begin to cover even these costs.

[47] H. Averch and L. Johnson, "Behavior of the Firm under Regulatory Constraint," *American Economic Review* vol. 52, no. 5 (December 1962) p. 1053.

[48] See for example, Joskow, "Inflation and Environmental Concern."

But before turning to those arguments, we must do for investment decisions in the metropolitan public utility services what we have done for pricing decisions; that is, examine the institutional and organizational determinants of present investment practices.

Effect of Regulation on Investment

The rules derived by economists for optimal provision of public utility services necessarily treat pricing and investment together. Perhaps the most startling feature of actual practice by firms and commissions is the extent to which pricing and investment decisions are made "independently." In the preceding discussion, we have surveyed public utility service practices in capacity requirement forecasting. Here the focus is on the relationship between the objectives of institutional actors in the provision process, the rules of the regulatory process, and the results of the capacity planning and provision process.

For these somewhat different purposes, it is important to recognize that some actors, in order to guarantee themselves a wider set of options, have strong incentives to separate the pricing and investment decisions. At one level, in which the regulatory commissions and the firms they regulate control demand only through price, the problem and the examples are tediously familiar, and the stereotypical institutional objectives are well known. Most familiar, perhaps, is the problem of urban limited-access highway investment. Few would contest the proposition that state highway departments wish to build as many highways as possible. They are constrained by the availability of revenues from state and federal trust funds, but federal funding of construction costs on a large scale considerably weakens that constraint. Capacity-planning practices, in order to effect "construction maximization," often reject intermodal cost-effectiveness comparisons (for example, a comparison of automobile traffic with limited-access bus transit), plan future capacity with extrapolations of past growth trends (especially if the recent past has been a rapid-growth period), and define the costs of highway construction as narrowly as possible.[49]

It is relatively easy—perhaps too easy—to suggest institutional solutions to these familiar problems. Whatever the practical constraints on

[49] See Anthony Downs, "Losses Imposed on Urban Households by Uncompensated Highway and Renewal Costs," in *Urban Problems and Prospects* (Chicago, Markham, 1970) p. 192–227.

changes in the governance of the public utility services, there is a persuasive case for changes in the direction of governance by multipurpose
elective bodies.[50] The argument is even more compelling, I believe, when
the public utility investment problem is seen as it actually appears in
the context of metropolitan growth problems. For metropolitan areas
have a range of devices—and not prices alone—for regulating demand,
and organizational incentives will shape the way in which metropolitan
jurisdictions employ those devices.

Consider, for example, the problems posed by staging policies, sometimes called growth-control, adequate public facilities, or capital improvements programs. (The last term often has a considerably broader
connotation, meaning any scheduling of capital facilities, not necessarily
one designed around any particular objective or set of objectives.)
Usually formal statements of the objectives of staging policies are broad,
even inconsistent, in their objectives. But there is enough of a family
resemblance that one may usefully be cited as an example.

. . . [The] uncoordinated growth of the past decade has created an im-
balance between population growth and economic development and has
limited the fiscal capability of the county to respond to the public service
needs of its residents. The Staging Policy proposes to coordinate private
development with public investment and to guide development of the county
in a proper sequential manner, so as to create a beneficial balance between
residential and employment opportunities. Specifically, the staging policy
addresses:

(1) establishment of a policy depicting areas recommended for develop-
    ment and areas recommended for preservation in the next decade,
(2) determination of the optimum rate of population growth and a proper
    balance between residential growth and economic development,
(3) development of population projections by geographic areas to be used
    as input in various county plans and programs, and
(4) determination in the amount of land needed to accommodate planned
    development of the next decade.[51]

Several objectives are apparent in this statement—the selection of an
optimum rate of population growth, the achievement of an optimal mix
between residences and employment and of an optimal mix between

[50] See E. Haefele, *Representative Government and Environmental Management*
(Baltimore, Johns Hopkins University Press for Resources for the Future, 1973).
[51] Prince Georges County, Maryland, *Proposed Staging Policy* (Maryland–
National Capital Park and Planning Commission and Prince Georges County
Planning Board, May 1973), inner cover and pp. 21–30.

development and preservation of open space. In addition, the plan states several means toward these ends, notably the development of improved population projections.

Of the stated objectives, some are central to the growth problem, and others are peripheral and not necessarily growth-related. In the first category is the relationship between fiscal capacity, the timing of public utility service investment, and population growth. Related to the problem of fiscal capacity, but somewhat peripheral to the staging problem, is the question of optimum mix between employment and residences, which in turn raises the question of fiscal zoning. And entirely peripheral to the problem of staging is the question of the optimum mix between development and open space, or between development and preservation. Therefore, our focus is on the relationship between fiscal capacity, population, and investment timing in such a way as to suggest guidelines for a positive theory of, and a normative appraisal of, staging policies.

In the typical staging problem, a local government or utility commission is obligated to, or decides to, provide increased capacity for the growing number of residents within its jurisdiction. The future course of population growth is known only uncertainly, yet the public utilities are required to provide some specific service, say, water and sewerage, for population growth as it occurs.

How will capacity be expanded, and how should capacity be expanded? The descriptive part of the problem is the easier one to solve: it depends upon the objectives and constraints facing the public authority or utility. The public facility staging literature usually treats the problem as one of minimizing discounted present cost. If population growth is known with certainty, the planning problem is one of timing investment so as to trade off the costs of carrying capacity greater than current demand against the cost savings associated with scale economies.[52] When population growth is uncertain, this method is extended by assuming some measure of public risk aversion against total present value of outlays, so that all project choices can be made at the same time.

There are two difficulties with using this formulation here, and both point to changes in our way of examining these policies. First, it is no

[52] See, for example, C. Russell, D. Arey, and R. Kates, *Drought and Water Supply* (Baltimore, Johns Hopkins University Press for Resources for the Future, 1970).

longer true that population growth is treated as exogenous in forecasting capacity requirements: for, with the advent of staging policies, the population variable—the timing and location of population increases within a jurisdiction—becomes a "control" variable. Second, on large projects the distributional effects can be sufficiently important that local governments simply balk at choosing between project alternatives on a discounted, present-value-of-cost basis.[53] For instance, project analyses show distinct patterns of costs over the project's lifetime—sometimes as long as several decades—and the costs are sometimes not negligible fractions of the jurisdictional tax base. Both of these difficulties point to the necessity of looking at local capacity planning in some context that allows explicit consideration of the spatial and temporal distributional effects of projects. The argument is strengthened by the need to trade and bargain, in these decisions, over a broader set than the individual public utility alternatives alone; and the need, argued above, to bring pricing and capacity decisions closer together.

An Electric Power Planning Model

Currently, I am developing a planning model for electric power capacity expansion in the Washington, D.C., SMSA. The model is substantially different, in several respects, from other work done on electric power. First, the demand side is extremely detailed—based on customer bills and load-curve data, so that the marginal rather than average price variables can be used and the choice between rate structural alternatives made a part of the capacity planning process. Further, jurisdictional population forecasts are integrated into demand forecasts, which depend not only upon average revenues but upon the rate structure. On the supply side, capacity expansion alternatives—including siting and generation mix—are both utilized. The model can be run for alternative parametric values of a shadow price of capacity shortfall, so that reserve margin decisions can be explicit. Either traditional, minimum present-value-of-cost criteria, or modifications of those criteria, which explicitly include distributional judgments,[54] can be used to select feasible solu-

[53] In a study done in cooperation with Montgomery County, Maryland, officials on the planning of wastewater treatment capacity expansion, we have found that such distributional effects can be substantial.

[54] These are based upon generalizations of M. Feldstein, "Equity and Efficiency in Public Sector Pricing: The Optimal Two-Part Tariff," *Quarterly Journal of Economics* vol. 86, no. 2 (May 1972) p. 175.

tions; but the point of the enterprise is to set out, in some reasonable detail, alternative capacity expansion and rate schedule time.

Those alternative time paths could, I believe, become the informational basis for a coherent public discussion of metropolitan electricity supply alternatives. Because those alternatives are interwoven with so many other pivotal metropolitan area choices, the forum would necessarily be one with metropolitanwide authority. In Washington, D.C., as in most metropolitan areas, there is no elective metropolitan authority; the closest thing to such an authority is the Council of Governments. It is possible that, over time, the council will evolve into some kind of metropolitan government, the impetus being the federal granting authority rather than any explicit local decision.[55]

Sidestepping the existence problem, how would a metropolitanwide government help in the governance of the electric power supply? The present framework of regulatory governance has been altered in several ways. The regulatory commission, presently the chartered creature of the state government, becomes the chartered creature of a metropolitan government. Its balancing functions—the functions summarized in what we called the shuttlecock commission—have been assigned to the metropolitan government, which must choose between the broad alternative policies and time paths set out by the commission. The commission is little more than a technically expert group working to set out those futures. Interest group pressures now must converge upon the metropolitan government and not upon the commission. The commission's models force trading on electricity supply alternatives within the metropolitan government to be trading among feasible alternatives, the distributional consequences of which are as explicit as the modeler's art can make them.

Optimistic? Perhaps, but not necessarily more so than the belief that the current regulatory commissions and the firms they regulate can be persuaded to act in accordance with economists' normative rules. Unrealistic? Again, it is possible, but not much more so than the assumption that the significant distributional implications of the major decision being made by present regulatory commissions can be neglected in the hope and the belief that all will come right in the long run.

[55] The EPA, for example, has chosen the Council of Governments (COG) as the sole area recipient of planning grants for wastewater treatment facilities, thus resolving a years-long interjurisdictional dispute (*Washington Post*, May 30, 1975).

5 / BARRY SCHECHTER

Taxes on Land Development: An Economic Analysis

FOR SOME TIME, local governments have made developers pay them a fee or tax for the right to develop particular parcels of land in specific ways. Earlier, developers had to pay in kind by providing certain facilities on the development site; however, the scope of the payment has since been enlarged. Now developers may have to provide access roads and, in certain cases, are required to dedicate land for use as parks or for schools. The latest stage in this process is the outright payment of cash fees to the local government. In some areas these funds are for a specific purpose; but in others the funds are not earmarked, and the purpose for which they are to be used is either vaguely defined or not defined at all.

Such requirements are becoming increasingly popular with local governments, and it is not difficult to see why. At a time of fiscal crisis in many urban areas and of considerable antigrowth feeling among existing residents, development fees provide both an additional source of revenue and a means of restricting growth. In this latter role, moreover, they have proved considerably more successful in the courts than have other antigrowth measures. To date, the only state courts of appeal or state supreme courts rulings against ordinances that require payments for new development have done so, not on constitutional grounds, but because the relevant governmental body lacked the necessary taxing authority. Thus, unless there is some reversal of this trend, in all probability we

The author, formerly at Resources for the Future, is with Barry Schechter Associates, Washington, D.C.

shall see more local governments introducing such measures and more state governments initiating legislation to permit them to do so.

In this chapter, I shall (1) consider arguments that may be made for the development tax from the perspective of the community which imposes it, (2) identify the gainers and the losers from the imposition of the tax, and (3) consider the implications of the tax from the standpoint of economic efficiency.

One argument for the tax on development is based on the protection of the interests of the current residents of the community in which the proposed development is to take place. It is assumed that the local government has the right to take measures to safeguard these interests, even where this may lower the welfare of outsiders who wish to enter the community. There are two lines to this argument: fiscal impacts and environmental effects.

FISCAL IMPACTS

The new development will add to both the receipts and expenditures of the local governments, and this is undoubtedly the primary motivation for the imposition of the tax. Each development is seen as a source of new revenues through the property tax payments of the homeowners and the new households, payment of various local income and sales taxes, as well as user charges. At the same time, the presence of new households will mean additional demands for public services such as fire protection, garbage collection, sewage disposal, parks, and schools, and this will necessitate higher local public expenditures.

In principle, any development project can therefore be classified as a "surplus" or "deficit" project, depending on whether the projected stream of additional receipts exceeds or falls short of the corresponding stream of additional costs. This kind of classification and some of its underlying assumptions and implications have given rise to a vast number of fiscal impact studies, which are designed to guide communities in their decisions about development. A more detailed analysis of such studies is the subject of chapter 2 (Ellman).

In this chapter, we are concerned with the argument for a development tax, which is based on this classification of deficit- and surplus-producing developments. If all developments are permitted, regardless of their fiscal impact on the community, the community will lose every time a deficit-producing project is undertaken. The additional demand placed on communal services will outpace the additional revenues, and in an effort to balance the budget services will have to be cut back or the rates of property or sales taxes, or both, will have to be raised on old *and* new residents. Thus, the new development must lower the welfare of the existing residents by subjecting them to deteriorating service quality or a rising tax rate.

In order to ensure that this does not take place, it is argued, the builder of the new development should be required to make good the shortfall in projected revenues through the development tax. By paying to the communal government an amount equal to the project deficit, he will thus enable the development to take place without straining local services or the taxing capacity of those already in the community. The avoidance of deficit development on the part of the local government has been termed *fiscal mercantilism.*

It should be noted that there are not many local communities which explicitly use this argument as a basis for their fees or taxes on development. However, Loudoun County, Virginia, has a charge that is to be imposed whenever there is a zoning change allowing for more intensive development. This charge is equal to the additional costs incurred by an increase in public services, after making some deductions for the future tax payments of the residents of the development.

There are several points to be made about this line of argument. First, it takes as its aim the protection of the welfare of those already in the community. Setting aside the question of whether the tax actually succeeds in realizing this aim, the argument raises the whole issue of the relationship between local communities and states and the total community. One of the problems of a federal system is the demarcation of jurisdiction, which raises questions of how far individual units such as states and local communities within that system can go in pursuing their own interests without regard to the welfare of those who live outside the community.

It obviously lies beyond the scope of this chapter to discuss the appropriate relationships that should exist between different parts of the federal system. The Supreme Court has, however, spoken to this issue, and one of its decisions bears an interesting relationship to the question of development taxes. In *Shapiro* v. *Thomson* [394 U.S. 618 (1969)], the Court ruled against the right of the City of New York to impose a one-year residency requirement on welfare recipients. Now, the imposition of such a requirement is analytically identical with the imposition on new residents who receive welfare of a tax equal to one year's welfare payments. The Court threw out the residency requirement because it restricted the recipient's right to travel. Certain decisions since then have narrowed somewhat the implications of that ruling, but the basic recognition of the principle remains. Similarly, in the *Petaluma* case in California, the federal district court ruled against the right of the City of Petaluma to restrict the amount of growth that could take place by actually prescribing a maximum number of dwellings in the community. Again, this ruling was based on the fact that an individual's right to travel was being restricted.[1]

Thus, the rights of individual communities to act in the interests of their own residents are certainly not absolute and have been subject to serious abridgement in this very field. Courts have recognized that certain local policies can adversely affect those now living outside who might wish to migrate into these communities. Whether the development tax being considered here would receive the same treatment in the courts as these previous cases remains an open question. It is certainly true, for example, that the Supreme Court, in other cases, has ruled in favor of a local community which acts to exclude outsiders. But the existence of a number of opposing decisions should give one pause before asserting, under all circumstances, the community's right to act in the interests of its current residents.

A second point should be made here: the specific argument that taxes on development protect the welfare of the current residents implies that the community currently is financing all of its needs, and that only the projected development will bring about a budget deficit at current tax rates. Thus, if no tax is imposed, the current residents will be called upon to subsidize new residents. The truth, however, is that the entire system of federal, state, and local government finances is riddled with subsidies, both within and between communities. For example, individuals pay sales and income taxes to the state, which then returns some

---

[1] However, the decision was later overturned on appeal.

of the revenues to local governments. Thus, a state effectively redistributes income among its different communities, using the funds collected from some communities to subsidize others. Similarly, the federal government collects revenues from individuals through the income tax and returns some of the revenues to the states in grants and revenue sharing. Once again, there is no reason to suppose that the moneys are returned in the proportion that they are collected. On the contrary, a definite redistribution is involved here. Thus, at every level, income is redistributed among different communities. To talk of old residents subsidizing the new residents within a community gives the impression that the old residents paid for themselves before the new residents moved in. It is just as likely that the old residents themselves are receiving an outside subsidy, and that their resistance to new households is based on their unwillingness to share this subsidy with newcomers.

ENVIRONMENTAL EFFECTS

The second part of the argument is concerned not so much with the flows of revenues and expenditures which new development generates, but with the environmental impact of this development. One suspects that this has not been the uppermost concern of those local governments which have attempted to impose some form of development tax, since their basic and immediate concern naturally has been with the budgets they have to control. Nevertheless, environmental quality is undoubtedly of some concern to local governments, and some fiscal impact studies do take serious account of the environmental effects of growth. Although these effects are not *financial*, in that they do not show up in any direct cash flow changes, they are nonetheless *economic*. That is, real costs and sacrifices of goods and services have to be made to deal with them, and if they are not dealt with, a real decline in the standard of living can result. An uncharitable interpretation of the environmental concern manifested by local governments is that such governments are willing to use the current national concern with the issue as a convenient instrument to reduce growth, which they oppose for other reasons.

In any event, new development can have an adverse environmental impact on the community in which it takes place, and it is of importance to examine this. Of paramount concern is the quality of the air we breathe. It is a commonplace that air quality is seriously affected by the volume of automobile traffic in a given area. Thus a residential development which will house families whose movement into the area will add significantly to the number of automobiles leads inevitably to a pollution of the air breathed by the population of the entire community. Water quality can be similarly affected by an increase in population; in this case, through the increased waste disposal that such an increase necessitates and the use of water supplies to effect this disposal. Clearly, the same analysis applies to the smoke and solid wastes generated by industrial development as well as the noise pollution and visual blight caused by certain kinds of haphazard development.

Land development, therefore, and the increase in the number of households and industrial undertakings which accompany it, can have an ill effect on the residents of the community. The effects will not show up *directly* in the community's budget, but may do so indirectly, for some will be driven out of the community, and their migration will affect the community's tax revenues, housing prices, and costs of public services. In estimating the well-being of different communities and the nation as a whole, we are accustomed to using some measure of money income deflated by some measure of the price level of goods and services purchased. But there is no way for this measure to capture the deterioration or improvement in the quality of the environment because we do not purchase environmental quality directly. It is associated with common property resources, which until recently have been treated as though they were free goods. Nonetheless, as we have belatedly begun to realize, the quality of the environment is an essential component of the standard of living, which has a real economic value, even if it is not associated in our minds with a financial transaction. Therefore, any measure of well-being which does not take some account of it must be considered defective.

It is important to decide whether to counteract the reduction in welfare caused by new development by a tax on that development. When we considered the fiscal effects of new development, there was no question of how the tax revenues would be used. The reason for collecting the tax in the first place was the shortfall in revenues as compared with the costs of augmented services for the new development. The tax revenues could therefore be used either to finance services which would otherwise be cut back, or to keep down tax rates which would otherwise have to rise, or, more probably, for some combination of the two. In the case of environmental quality, however, the problem is not one of budget balancing. The costs of which we are speaking do not show up directly in the budget but are experienced as a deterioration in the quality of goods that are not usually directly exchanged for money in private or public markets. How, therefore, would the tax revenues be used?

There are two possible answers to this question, applicable to different kinds of environmental damage. The proceeds could be used, first of all, to construct facilities for maintaining or improving environmental quality, where this is technically possible. For example, improved treatment plants for water could help to offset the deterioration in quality caused by increased household and industrial demands. Thus, the quality enjoyed by the old residents of the community would therefore not decline. This use of the development tax revenues corresponds to the use of tax revenues to maintain public service standards in the case of adverse fiscal impact.

There are, however, cases where it may be technically impossible to repair the environmental damage that has been done, for example, when the appearance of an entire neighborhood has been changed for the worse or when such improvements would be too costly. Here, the tax revenues could be used to make a direct payment to the residents who had suffered as compensation for the diminution of their welfare. In the case of adverse fiscal impact, this corresponds with the use of tax revenues to reduce any tax increases on the old residents that would otherwise be necessary. In both cases a money payment is made to the adversely affected residents, in one case directly and in the other by reduction of their tax bills.

There is also the question of whether the communal government will find it in its own interest to confine the tax to the purpose for which it has been publicly announced. Even if the tax were officially designated for the purpose of discouraging environmentally damaging developments, the local government will have every incentive to raise the tax as high as possible, in order to keep out all new developments. Without impugning the integrity of those who perform studies for various public bodies, all such reports contain a certain element of advocacy. They are all written for a particular point of view, and to some extent their estimates of environmental damage are flexible. Determinations are made as to which factors can be safely omitted and which must be included, and the final figures always depend on certain crucial assumptions about which the layman is unlikely to be sophisticated. With a government pushing for a particular outcome, and the underlying research having the capability of producing a variety of outcomes, one can only expect that the final tax figure would exceed rather than fall short of compensating for the "true" damage that development causes to the environment.

Let us now consider the underlying assumption that it is the *development* which somehow causes the environmental deterioration, and the tax on that development—by reducing the volume of development and raising funds for expenditures to offset the damage incurred from the development—which therefore protects the current residents from the deterioration. This is undoubtedly true of the physical characteristics of the building itself: for, if the buildings are ugly, there is no question that it is the development itself which is the cause of the trouble.

Most of the effects discussed, however, are not direct consequences of the development, but of the activity of its residents. Here we should make a distinction between uses and activities which are discretionary and those that are more or less fixed or forced. A certain number of people living in a particular area are bound to create a certain amount of waste materials. Insofar as these materials have to be disposed of in given ways, the existence of the development is bound to lead to a fixed amount of environmental deterioration.

But in, say, the use of the automobile, people exercise a choice as to how much travel they will undertake, and whether it will be by public or private transportation. Therefore, there is no necessary relationship between a given number of residents and a given amount of air pollution from automobile use. The relationship depends on a host of other factors, such as the distance from one's residence to work, the existence of good alternative public transportation, the available network of free and toll roads, and so forth. Since, therefore, people have a choice of using an automobile for certain trips and not for others, is it not more rational to charge for these trips, rather than to tax the developer for all the projected pollution that will occur from future residents' automobile use?

And if it is rational to ask that new residents pay for their automobile use, why should the old residents not have to pay similarly? This, of course, undermines the attempt to protect the old residents from the bad consequences of the new development, and it highlights an important but seldom considered fact about the supposed ill effects of new development upon environmental quality.

This is that all households, new *and* old, are responsible for degrading the environment. The impression is sometimes given that only new residents use sewage facilities and drive automobiles which pollute the air and crowd the highways. Underlying an argument for a development tax based on environmental damage must be the assumption that the old households have more right to live in their community than the new.

Thus, while environmental damage is of serious consequence, and it is difficult to see how a totally free market could possibly solve the problems that it brings, the use of a development tax, assessed and levied by local communities, is not the means by which we can solve this particular problem.

TAX INCIDENCE

So far, we have implicitly accepted the view that a development tax, while possibly harming would-be in-migrants, protects the welfare of the old residents in the community. In fact, certain groups of these residents will be harmed economically by the imposition of this tax. The reason for this is that the final incidence of the burden of the tax, like that of any tax, is very different from its immediate impact. In this section I analyze the question of the incidence of the tax, and attempt to identify the gainers and losers *within* the community.

There are two facts about the development tax which must be taken into account in this analysis. First, it is levied in the market for housing in particular jurisdictions. The resident pays for accommodation but in turn receives not only accommodation but also a particular package of publicly provided goods and services, which he shares with the other residents of this jurisdiction. Second, the situation is one of change rather than equilibrium. Much of traditional incidence theory is concerned with a market where the variables initially have no tendency to change. A tax is then levied, introducing the change which is the subject of analysis. Here, there is a disturbance which precedes and, indeed, provokes the levying of the tax. It is the growth in community size from in-migration which causes the jurisdictional government to seek additional sources of revenue by this tax.

The increased demand for residential accommodation which arises from in-migration to a jurisdiction raises the price of accommodation and increases the size of the community. The question is, By how much? The effect of the impact tax is to keep the community from growing as fast as it otherwise would, and to make the price of accommodation rise *more* than it otherwise would. This applies to the price of *all* housing.

How does this come about? In the first place, as has been noted, the impulse for imposing such a tax arises from a growth in the demand for accommodation through in-migration. There are, of course, other sources of growth. The community itself can grow through natural increase, which can be reflected in the number of households seeking accommodation. Whatever the source of the increased demand for accommodation, it results in a shortage of housing at current prices. This drives up the price and gives developers an incentive to build new houses or apartments to meet the increased demand.

To determine the consequences of the tax, we must contrast the reaction of the housing market to the excess demand in the presence or absence of the tax. To do this, we must specify the behavior of the jurisdictional government when it does not levy a development tax. The reason for levying such a tax is the presumed inability of the community to maintain the current level of public services for the expanded population, even with the additional revenues that such a population increase will bring through property, sales, and income taxes, and various user charges. In that case, with no development tax, either the quality of public services will have to be cut, or the rates on some other existing taxes will have to be raised, or some combination of the two must occur. When we talk of the effect of the development tax, therefore, we must specify the actions that the government will take in the absence of the tax, in order to be able to make the correct comparison.

First, let us assume that the quality of public services will be maintained. This means that with no development tax, more revenues will have to be raised from some other source. Let us also assume that this revenue source is within the jurisdiction—that is, that it receives no extra assistance from outside, such as from the state and federal governments. The main difference, then, between financing the services from the development tax and some other internal tax, is that the other tax will not discriminate between new and old accommodations. The principal feature of the development impact tax is that it is a tax on new accommodation alone. It is not directly paid by the owners of existing property. Any other tax applies to new and old alike, even though it may use some other basis for discrimination, such as the value of property or the household's level of income.

Thus, the alternatives being compared are raising a given revenue from (1) a development tax on new housing alone, and (2) an increase in the rate of a tax on all residents or property owners in the jurisdiction. Since it is levied on a smaller base, the development tax must be at a higher rate, in order to raise the same revenue. Its effect is to subject new housing to a higher rate of tax than would otherwise be the case. This, then, will slow down growth and increase the cost of new housing by more than would otherwise be the case. I shall deal with the two effects separately.

First, I will discuss a higher rate of tax on new accommodation. The builder has to pay the development tax himself and, as a consequence, will try to pass on the whole of this increase to the buyer. The buyer has less property tax to pay once he owns the house, but, as we have seen, this saving is far less than the additional cost of the development tax. Therefore, the demand for new houses will fall. Households which would have bought in this location will now buy elsewhere. Either they will buy outside the jurisdiction, where no tax of this kind has been imposed, or they will try to buy existing houses in that part of the jurisdiction where there is no development tax. The effect of this buying pattern will moderate somewhat the initial price increase. Thus, the ultimate increase in the price of new houses will be less than the full amount of the tax.

Since, however, there are some households that now demand accommodation in those areas having older houses, the prices for the older housing will also rise. Although the effect of this demand may take longer to register, it will still be felt.

This, then, represents the effect of the net increase in the tax on the new houses. But we also must take into account the reduction in the tax paid by those members of the community living in older houses. However, this will have relatively little effect, assuming that the reduction takes place within the rates of property tax. The property tax rate reduction may encourage certain owners to take better care of their property, and hence prolong its life. Thus, in the long run, the supply of housing may be increased somewhat by the reduction. But this is a long-term effect, and it is also probably of little magnitude; certainly so, when compared with the direct and immediate reduction in supply caused by the higher rate of impact tax. Moreover, in those communities considering or attempting to impose impact taxes, the government's immediate problems are ones of rapid growth rather than the long-run provision of housing.

Thus, when compared with a jurisdiction having the same provision of public goods, the effect of the tax is to reduce the size of the community below what it would be without the tax,[2] and to raise the price of all accommodation. Since the demand for accommodation is rising regardless of the tax structure, causing a rise in the price of accommodation and an increase in the size of the community, we can see that the effect of the development tax is to raise the price still further but to moderate the increase in the size of the community.

Who benefits from the tax and who loses? We know for certain that the demand for new accommodation falls. Some households look for accommodation elsewhere because of the tax, whereas in its absence they would have preferred to live in a new accommodation in the jurisdiction which imposes the tax. They sustain a loss, the size of which depends upon the numbers who are turned away by this price increase, and how much less they like the alternatives they choose.

Who among the long-term residents of the community gains and who loses? This question is more difficult to answer, since they face both changes in tax rates (property tax rates) and changes in the net price of accommodation. One group, however, certainly loses—the households which leave the community, having lived there before, because of the rise in the price of accommodation. If this increase had not taken place, they would have remained in the community, but now they are forced to seek an inferior, but less costly, alternative outside.

Residents who remain in the jurisdiction are faced with higher rents than they would otherwise have to pay, although the quality of the public services they enjoy remains the same. Those who have always rented

---

[2] The argument must be qualified, but in no way that affects its substance. We have been assuming the same quality of public goods provision, but have been arguing for the case of the same total *revenue*. If the development tax does indeed reduce community size, a smaller revenue will be required. Thus the tax on development will have to be less than we have assumed, but it will still be greater than the rise in the property tax rate would have to be.

accommodations there but are not homeowners, also face a loss in welfare. The only group that can gain are the owners of accommodations. The rents they receive rise, while their tax bills are less than they would have been if no impact taxes were imposed. Thus, a household which both owns a house *and* lives in it makes a net gain. It pays no rent to itself, so there is no change on that score, but its property tax bill is reduced, while the quality of services it enjoys is unchanged.

This set of results is somewhat surprising. It indicates that the simple lineup of interests that one might imagine from a superficial analysis of the problem is not the one which, in fact, is relevant. The simple analysis leads one to believe that the interests of the present residents of the community are directly opposed to those living outside who wish to enter. We have seen how wrong this is. The question remains as to why this conclusion is wrong.

To understand this, we must consider what happens when the demand for any commodity rises. In the usual case of a rising supply curve, the effect is to raise both the price and the quantity supplied. Those using the commodity before the price rise are now worse off than they were before, since they must now pay more for the same thing. Any attempt to reduce the number of new users by taxing certain suppliers only worsens the situation of the former users. In addition to having to compete with the new users, they are limiting the supply of this commodity, which means that they have to compete for an even smaller supply, which in turn serves to drive up the price.[3]

ALLOCATIVE EFFICIENCY

In this section I consider the argument for a development tax from the standpoint of the efficiency of the entire U.S. economy rather than from the interests of any particular group. Households choose a location on the basis of its proximity to work, the costs of accommodation, transportation, taxation, and so forth. If these costs and returns also represent

[3] I am aware that this conclusion ignores the reduction in the property tax. But this will always have less effect in increasing supply than the development tax will have in diminishing it. The one exception to this that I can discover is the case in which (1) the reduction in the property tax is expected to continue so that the present value of the house initially rises by some multiple of the tax reduction, and (2) the rate of growth of the community is greater than this multiple rate of interest.

the costs and returns to society as a whole, the household's freedom to choose any location would lead to an efficient allocation of households in different areas. By choosing the location with the highest net private return, the individual would ensure that he was being productive, and thus that the economy worked efficiently.

But this does not work in practice, so the argument runs, since in making a decision about residential location, the household imposes costs on others which it fails to account for in its own calculations of the costs and benefits. For example, a household moving into a crowded urban area, where public services are sufficient to serve only the existing households, inflicts additional costs on those households. Either they find their services effectively cut back through overcrowding, or they must pay for the expansion of the service to serve the new residents. At the same time, as we have seen, additional public expenditures may be necessary to maintain environmental quality. The assumption here is, of course, that extra revenue raised from the new residents at the current rate of taxation is insufficient to pay for this. In deciding to locate here, the new resident is not faced with this cost, even though he imposes it. For example, if a household has the choice between two different places of residence, and the net return when living in location A is $18,000 a year, while the net return when living in location B is $17,000, it will choose to live and work in A. If no other costs were imposed, this would also be in the interests of the efficiency of the whole economy. But say that community A must raise an additional $2,000 to maintain the quality of the environment and the level of public services, whereas community B can do so with no extra revenue. In that case economic efficiency requires the household to locate in B, not A. Although the private return from the point of view of the household is greater in A, the total return from the point of view of society is greater in B. Although the private return to the household is less in location B, the external cost, or the cost imposed on others is less too, and by a greater amount.

The incentives facing the individual do not ensure that his free decision brings about an efficient outcome for the economy as a whole. In order to correct the incentives, it is necessary to impose additional taxes on new development, so that the household will have to pay the true cost of residing in an area. In this way, the private returns from living in different areas will correspond to the social returns, and the free decisions of individual households as to their location will once more lead to an economically efficient outcome for the overall economy.

Such is the argument for development taxes from external effects: in order to appraise its validity, we must distinguish carefully between various kinds of effects. We have already seen the disadvantages of the tax as an instrument for the correction of environmental external effects. Let us therefore consider the different possible sources of the harmful fiscal impacts. We shall see that there are really two forces at work here, and we must draw a fundamental distinction between them.

First, when the demand for any commodity or services rises, its price rises in consequence. This gives an incentive to users to cut down on their demands, and to suppliers to produce more. In the longer run the price may fall, if the expansion in output allows for economies of scale or a more efficient organization of production, possibly through the discovery of better techniques. But the long-run supply curve of the industry may also slope upward. In this case, even after supply has had time to adjust to the new level of demand, the price will remain higher than it was before the demand curve shifted.

Our knowledge of the cost conditions underlying the production of local services, such as those previously mentioned, is limited. But what we do know makes it likely that the long-run supply curve of such services is upward-sloping.[4] Insofar as they are literally service industries, they are precisely the industries in which the opportunities for productivity increases are most limited. Moreover, experience has shown that when governments reach a certain size, public employees become unionized, and can press more effectively for wage increases. For a very small community, it is possible that certain economies of scale may be realized, since there can be a minimum size of plant for certain undertakings below which it would be uneconomical to build. But in the majority of cases, the unit cost of providing public services will rise with the scale of services provided.

A second reason for the increased cost of services to the local government is that publicly provided services rarely charge their customers according to the use they make of the service. In some cases it may be technically impossible to do so; in others, the cost of calculating such prices may be prohibitive. For some services, it is a matter of policy that it would be wrong to charge for them on the basis of use, since any such

[4] See Werner Z. Hirsch, *Urban Economic Analysis* (New York, McGraw-Hill, 1973).

fee would bear especially hard on low-income families, and the service should be available to all, regardless of means. The argument then is based on the objective of redistributing income.

Whatever the reason in any particular case, the result is that a whole array of services are financed not by charges levied directly on the users in the community and varying with their use, but by taxing the whole community. Therefore, this arrangement calls for those who are relatively highly taxed but relatively light users of the services to subsidize those who are relatively lightly taxed but relatively high users of the services. One dramatic example of this is schooling. Large poor families, occupying property with a low assessed value, make heavy use of the public schools but pay relatively little in property taxes. On the other hand, those who have few or no children make little or no use of the public schools; yet they must contribute to the running of those services through a possibly higher tax bill.

Since some households in the community are subsidizing others when there is movement into and out of a community, the level of subsidies changes. An influx of poor households which make heavy use of public services will add to the number receiving subsidies. Therefore, if there is no increase in tax rates, the average standard of public services must decline.

Aside from the subsidization and redistribution that goes on *within* the community in this way, the same phenomenon occurs among communities, as has been mentioned previously. It is totally misleading to speak of the old residents of the community as subsidizing the new. In reality, there is a complicated system of subsidies among and within communities, and the expansion of the community through the addition of new households changes this in a way which may lower the standards enjoyed by the old members of the community. But the reason is equally likely to be that the old members of the community were themselves enjoying a subsidy which they now have to share with more people.

In any event, this is what lies behind the decline in standards faced by an expanding community. The system of subsidies within and among communities increases the price that members of the community have to pay, even though there has been no change in the real cost of public services. On the other hand, an increased cost of services can come about because of the rise in the output of those services, and means that the per unit of cost of such services is now higher.

Having distinguished the two totally different causes of the drop in the standards of living enjoyed by old members of the community, we are now in a position to consider which of them, if either, demands some kind of correction by the government in order to prevent the external effect from distorting incentives for residential location in such a way that economic efficiency will be harmed. Let us consider first the rise in price which stems from the increase in real cost. When the increased demand for a private good raises its price, it is not normally argued that the government should intervene. Why then should it intervene when the same happens to a publicly provided good? If this were the only reason for increases in the price of services, there would be no distortion of incentives for residential location. On the contrary, the introduction of a tax on development, making it more expensive to live in such an area, would itself introduce a distortion by making it too expensive to develop new residential buildings in the area. Therefore, this is no argument for a tax on new developments.

The second reason for price increases in public services is, however, the fiscal arrangements of various governments. It is these arrangements, whatever their justification on other grounds, that lead to a diminution of standards for the older members of the community. Thus, the distortions which arise on this account are fiscally induced and may give people the wrong incentives to live in different areas.

Once we realize that an important part of the inefficiency, which is supposed to exist in this context, is due to the action of the government itself, we must also take into account the reason why the government takes such measures in the first place. The basis for these decisions is the redistribution of income between individuals and communities. Whenever this is done, and by whatever means, inefficiencies will be introduced. That is the price that must be paid for such redistribution. The inefficiencies arising from any redistribution should be kept to a minimum, however. To this end, numerous changes in the present system have been proposed, which generally embody either or both of two features: The programs are federally run, or they substitute cash benefits for benefits in kind. But it is at once apparent that the local development tax has neither feature. Nor is it surprising to learn that it has never been proposed as a means of reconciling efficiency with redistribution. It is not possible to accomplish this by adding yet another local tax to the already existing ones.

SUMMARY AND CONCLUSION

We have considered arguments for the development tax from two points of view and found both of them wanting.

First, we considered the argument that the tax was in the interests of the residents of the community which imposes it, and that it has a right to take measures to protect those interests. The value judgment underlying the assertion of this right is one that has been questioned, especially in the light of the fact that different communities are bound together by redistribution schemes among and within each other. But quite aside from any value judgment, we have demonstrated that the view of the tax as a protector of the local community interests is in error. In fact, the renters of residential accommodation, new or old, in the community will lose by this tax. It will discourage the supply of new accommodation, thus driving up the price of all accommodation.

We then considered the argument from a broader point of view—that of the efficiency of the operation of the economy as a whole. We discovered that, with no tax of this kind and with the current system of provision of local services and their financing, two sources of inefficiency could be identified. One was itself the result of governmental action in providing services free or below cost, while raising the revenues for this in such a way as to effectively redistribute income among and within communities. By having to pay less than the market price for services, the households' incentives to reside in different areas will not correspond to their social cost. This, however, is a consequence of any scheme under which general tax revenues are raised to subsidize specific services. Any redistribution of income such as this can only be bought at the cost of some economic inefficiency. It is, of course, the task of economic policy to obtain the desired redistribution with a minimum of inefficiency, but imposing a special tax on new development in no way has contributed to this goal.

The second source of inefficiency does not stem from governmental action but is a consequence of the technology we use. Broadly speaking, that source is what is referred to as an environmental cost, and what would be classified as a technical external diseconomy by economists. There is no question that the presence of this phenomenon lessens the efficiency of the economy, but the imposition of a development tax will not necessarily make it any more efficient, or take us closer to the ideal. Some of the so-called environmental costs of development are not costs of the development itself, but are the result of the actions of the development residents, actions which in themselves are discretionary and which are also taken by other residents. If any tax is appropriate to correct this inefficiency, it should be a tax on these discretionary actions, no matter who takes them. In principle, the costs which are associated with the development itself are candidates for taxation, but in practice the administrative and political arguments against them are overwhelming. For example, even if all members of a community agree that a certain style of building is ugly, it is not feasible to determine the monetary value of their revulsion and to levy a tax equal to this on the builder of such a building, or to reimburse the members of the community where the building is located. The temptation will be great to use the tax simply as a means of excluding all buildings that the community decides it does not want.

Therefore, we must conclude that the levying of a development tax cannot be justified.

6 / J. MICHAEL CUMMINS

Local Government Finance
and the Regulated Firm

OVER THE LAST SEVERAL YEARS, the principal financial problem faced by metropolitan governments has been that the demand for the public goods and services they provide has been growing rapidly, while the tax base used to finance these services has not been keeping pace. More specifically, within the metropolitan area the central cities have exhibited a high concentration of poverty, people, and buildings. This gives rise to high per capita demands for public assistance (welfare), police and fire protection, sanitation facilities, and public education. Also, the inflow of commuters from the surrounding suburbs creates additional demands for public services provided by the cities. The growing disparity between expenditures and revenues is principally the result of the higher-income population moving to the suburbs, with retail stores and manufacturing firms following in their wake. The financial problem is further compounded by a fragmented structure of local government jurisdictions throughout most metropolitan areas, which largely prevents central cities from tapping revenue sources located in the surrounding suburbs. All this has resulted in the application of higher tax rates to the eroding central city tax base and deteriorating public services.[1]

At the same time that inadequate revenues have prevented metropolitan governments from satisfying the increasing expenditure demands

The author is an assistant professor of business economics, Graduate School of Business, Stanford University.

[1] J. F. Due, and A. F. Friedlaender, *Government Finance: Economics of the Public Sector* (5th ed., Homewood, Ill., Richard D. Irwin, 1973) pp. 507–512.

of their constituents, there has been a growing trend toward the private provision of public goods and services which usually are supplied collectively through the public sector of the economy. This activity has been observed under the guise of the social responsibility of business or corporate philanthropy. Until recently, the general feeling was that a firm's only responsibility was to make profits for its owners.

However, recent years have seen a growing public demand for social responsibility on the part of private firms, and this has sparked a large controversy over the appropriate role of the modern corporation in society.[2] Whatever the final outcome, it seems clear that public opinion concerning corporate involvement in social activities has changed substantially. This suggests that public sentiment perhaps now favors the idea of having private firms rather than government supply at least some public goods and services. If this is so, and it is assumed that firms are not acting altruistically in providing these services, it is important to understand the mechanism by which firms receive remuneration for supplying these services, and to determine whether the allocation of resources resulting from private provision is efficient and equitable.

In an attempt to assess the actual and potential impact of the private provision of public goods and services, it is my purpose in this chapter to (1) examine empirically the extent of this phenomenon with respect to regulated firms, (2) construct a positive model of the process within a collective choice framework, and (3) to normatively assess the allocative effects of such activities.[3, 4]

[2] See J. W. McKie, ed., *Social Responsibility and the Business Predicament.* (Washington, D.C., Brookings Institution, 1974); S. P. Sethi, ed., *The Unstable Ground: Corporate Social Policy in a Dynamic Society* (Los Angeles, Melville, 1974); and M. R. Freemont-Smith, *Philanthropy and the Business Corporation* (New York, Russell Sage, 1972).

[3] The focus of the analysis on regulated firms is prompted by the fact that almost all firms are operating under some form of regulatory constraint. Furthermore, it is felt that the mechanism by which firms are remunerated for providing public goods and services involves public policy outcomes favorable to the firm, which can be conveniently expressed as the incremental relaxation of the regulatory constraints under which the firm operates.

[4] W. J. Samuels, ["Externalities, Rate Structure, and the Theory of Public Utility Regulation," in Harry M. Trebing, ed., *Essays on Public Utility Pricing and Regulations* (East Lansing, Mich., Michigan State University, 1971)], building on previously espoused social principles of public utility pricing [See J. C. Bonbright, *Principles of Public Utility Rates* (New York, Columbia University Press, 1961) pp. 109–120], has advocated a very limited use of public utilities as a mechanism for helping to solve urban problems. He feels their potential use is quite restricted

EMPIRICAL BACKGROUND

Corporate philanthropy takes many different forms and is accounted for in different ways, making accurate quantitative data on these activities difficult to obtain. Even though charitable contributions made by corporations are supposedly reported on income tax returns, surveys have indicated that it is common practice to record many charitable gifts as ordinary business expenses rather than actual contributions. Moreover, the amounts recorded on tax returns do not reflect the full value of personnel services and other contributions-in-kind underwritten by the firm. In addition, programs more recently undertaken to solve urban problems, to improve the environment, and to support cultural activities, etc., are not usually included under corporate charitable contributions.

Keeping these limitations in mind, information obtained from corporaate balance sheet statements indicates that the reported percentage of net income before taxes going to charitable contributions has risen from 0.31 percent during the period 1936–40 to 1.28 percent for 1969–70.[5] Table 6-1 shows a breakdown, by industry class, of the corporate contributions for 1969–70, as reported on income tax returns. The total value of contributions recorded was just over $1 billion, with the majority coming from manufacturing firms.

In attempting to assess the role of the more stringently regulated firms in supplying charitable contributions, it seems reasonable to expect that they would fall within the categories of transportation, communication, electric, gas, and sanitary services or finance, insurance, and real estate. These groups together accounted for just over 21 percent of total corporate contributions, or about $224 million. From this data, it seems reasonable to conclude that the regulated industries are currently contributing to philanthropic activities in a manner consistent with business as a whole, even though the actual amounts involved are not large. In fact, relative to total local government expenditures on public goods and services, the contributions of regulated firms are miniscule—only 0.3 percent of general direct expenditures of all local governments in 1969–

---

because utility rates reflecting the cost of social programs would distort the allocation of resources by conflicting with efficient pricing based on a cost-of-service criterion. Also, Samuels argues that it would be extremely difficult for public utilities to adequately assess the costs and benefits of various social programs in order to efficiently decide which ones to undertake.

⁵ See Freemont-Smith, *Philanthropy*, pp. 31–35, and table 6-1. ·

TABLE 6-1. Corporation Contributions: Amount and Percentage of Net Profit by Industrial Groups, All Active Corporations, 1969–70 (in thousands of dollars)

Industrial group	Number of corporations	Net profit (total receipts less total deductions)	Contributions		
			Amount	Percentage of total	Percentage of net profit
Total	1,658,820	82,134,774	1,055,370	100.00	1.28
Agriculture, forestry, and fisheries	31,979	257,972	2,888	0.27	1.12
Mining	14,028	1,545,016	8,329	0.79	0.54
Contract construction	127,670	1,660,480	25,321	2.40	1.52
Manufacturing	202,102	40,385,611	614,378	58.21	1.52
Transportation, communication, electric, gas, and sanitary services	66,945	10,068,289	92,470	8.76	0.92
Transportation	51,967	895,163	22,245	2.11	2.48
Communication	6,870	4,962,341	30,590	2.90	0.62
Electric, gas, and sanitary services	8,108	4,210,785	39,635	3.76	0.94
Wholesale and retail trade	524,586	10,728,457	152,004	14.40	1.42
Finance, insurance, and real estate	428,872	15,831,686	131,379	12.45	0.83
Services	261,640	1,654,496	28,512	2.70	1.72
Not allocable	898	2,767	89	0.01	3.22

Source: Statistics of Income . . . 1969, Corporation Income Tax Returns. Accounting periods ending July 1969 through June 1970. (Washington, D.C., U.S. Govt. Print. Off., 1973) pp. 14–19.

70.[6] However, these expenditures by firms are growing over time and, given the changing public attitude toward the social responsibility of business, may one day be quite large. Also, these contributions recorded on tax returns constitute only a fraction of the total range and magnitude of public service activities undertaken by regulated firms.

In fact, beginning in the mid-sixties, a shift took place in the structure of corporate philanthropic activity, with much greater emphasis being placed upon civic causes, and special attention being given to minority groups and urban problems. This change represents both the addition of new funds over and above that given in the past to other causes, as well as shifts of funds previously allocated to traditional philanthropic activities.[7] Moreover, in addition to actual cash contributions, many firms have instituted minority group-hiring programs; training, upgrading, and hiring programs for the hard-core unemployed as well as donating staff, executive time, facilities, and equipment to help solve urban problems.

In a survey of 247 major corporations, taken in the late sixties, it was found that while certain industries take the lead in providing specific types of social programs designed to deal with the various urban problems, the regulated firms (that is, banks, utilities, and insurance companies) were in the forefront with respect to most, if not all, of the programs undertaken. Table 6-2 gives some indication of the extent to which various types of firms undertake these kinds of programs.[8] Let us now turn to some specific examples.

In the counties of northern Virginia (part of the Washington, D.C., metropolitan area), it is common practice for land developers to donate land to the county for parks and school sites, or to offer to build roads, etc., in exchange for receiving favorable county rulings on development proposals and applications for rezoning to higher density (which favors the developer through lower development costs). In Fairfax County, Virginia, it is estimated that a school site is worth from $200,000 to $300,000; and as of June 1973, approximately fifty school site donations had been made or were pending.[9]

[6] Tax Foundation, Inc., *Facts and Figures on Government Finance: 1975* (New York, Tax Foundation, Inc., 1975).
[7] See Freemont-Smith, *Philanthropy,* pp. 47–53.
[8] J. Cohn, "Is Business Meeting the Challenge of Urban Affairs?," *Harvard Business Review* (March-April 1970) pp. 70–72.
[9] T. Ellman, "Development Fees in Northern Virginia Counties." (July 1974) pp. 4–6.

TABLE 6-2. Extent of Corporate Involvement in Programs Designed to Solve Urban Problems

Industry class	Number of firms surveyed	Percentage of companies involved			
		Corporate donations program	Hard-core hiring	Special minority hiring, training and upgrading programs	Hard-core training and upgrading
Aerospace, aircraft	15	50	72	80	38
Banks	14	100	50	59	39
Building materials	13	28	15	29	0
Chemicals	13	38	0	30	0
Electronics, appliances	20	65	49	49	26
Farm and industrial machinery	8	20	9	26	0
Food and beverage	18	60	25	35	0
Insurance	39	70	48	81	27
Merchandising	15	80	25	60	0
Metal manufacturing and metal products	8	25	0	25	0
Motor vehicles and parts	8	42	75	100	51
Office machinery, computers	6	58	59	75	51
Petroleum	30	50	12	50	5
Scientific and photographic equipment	6	50	50	75	28
Transportation	9	50	15	60	15
Utilities	11	78	52	59	30
Other	14	50	30	59	12
Total number of firms surveyed	247				

Source: Jules Cohn, "Is Business Meeting the Challenge of Urban Affairs?" Harvard Business Review (March–April 1970) pp. 71–72, exhibit II.

The CBS television network finances a weekly half-hour program, "Opportunity Line," which is shown on CBS-owned TV stations in Chicago, Los Angeles, New York, Philadelphia, Saint Louis, and nineteen other cities. The program is a minority recruiting device, which describes job openings, demonstrates job interview situations, and counsels viewers on how to apply. A battery of interviewers from the state employment service takes the calls from viewers inquiring about these jobs.[10]

[10] The Conference Board, Business Amid Urban Crisis: Private-Sector Approaches to City Problems (New York, National Industrial Board, Inc., 1968) p. 4.

Michigan Bell Telephone Co. is very active in helping to solve metropolitan area problems within the state of Michigan. They utilize a mobile employment trailer in minority group areas of several Michigan cities to search for underprivileged potential employees. They have effectively adopted Detroit's Northern High School by donating the following services to them:

1. Running of a five-week employment readiness course for seniors and a Saturday training project on telephony
2. Making financial contributions earmarked to help Northern graduates needing such aid for college
3. Extending technical help to journalism students from personnel of the Michigan Bell Co. newspaper
4. Providing educational programs by Bell
5. Making available the services of a Bell employment interviewer as business consultant and aide to school counselors.

In addition, as a public service, Michigan Bell has compiled, printed, and distributed a directory of all law enforcement officials in Michigan. Furthermore, the company contributes executive time and makes financial donations to both the capital and operating budgets of the Detroit Educational Television Foundation—an organization designed to promote the cultural, educational, and civic welfare of the citizens of the community.[11]

Finally, the Pacific Gas and Electric Co., located in northern California, has devised a program, "A Congress for Community Progress," which is designed to assist cities and towns in its service area analyze community problems and then take steps to solve them. In addition to developing the program, Pacific Gas and Electric provides the advisory and promotional staffs, as well as follow-up services, to those communities interested in the program.[12]

This evidence suggests that regulated firms are indeed attempting to provide at least some portion of the total quantity of public goods and services demanded in metropolitan areas. This leads to the inevitable question of why this phenomenon is occurring. On what basis is the seeming philanthropic provision of public goods and services by private firms rationally explained? Furthermore, given that this phenomenon is

[11] Ibid., pp. 4, 22, 34, and 44.
[12] Ibid., p. 54.

occurring, should public policy be designed to discourage or encourage this type of behavior on the part of private firms? The rest of this chapter will be devoted to the development of a framework for answering these questions and the establishment of some guidelines for public policy decisions regarding these activities.

THE BASIC MODEL

In attempting to construct a model of the private provision of public goods and services, it is assumed that, in general, private firms are *not* behaving altruistically but are acting solely in the pursuit of profit. However, this raises the question of how the private firm can be expected to earn additional profits by supplying public goods and services without receiving direct remuneration. In general, it is not clear from the empirical evidence presented above how the firm is being compensated for the provision of these goods and services. It is conceivable that the firm could be increasing its profitability by stimulating demand for its private product through such philanthropic activity; however, it seems unlikely that this method of indirect remuneration alone could account for the wide range of these activities and the extensive involvement of many private firms.

Another way in which the firm might be indirectly compensated would be through public policy decisions which favorably influence the firm's operating environment. Almost all firms operate under some form of publicly imposed regulatory constraint (or the direct threat of regulatory intervention); consequently, it would be in the firm's interest to provide public goods and services in exchange for public policy decisions designed to alter in a compensatory manner the network of regulatory constraints under which the firm operates.

A clear example of this type of indirect compensation is the case of land development in northern Virginia, described above. Here the private firm (a developer) is providing public goods and services (parks, roads, school sites) in exchange for a compensatory relaxation of the regulatory constraints under which it operates (that is, zoning laws, building permits, and other land development regulations).

It is implicit in the compensatory relaxation of regulatory constraints faced by the firm that the collective choice process has sanctioned these public service activities of the private firm by providing remuneration in this manner. Therefore, if the collective choice mechanism by which public policy decisions are made can be assumed to be reasonably effective in representing individual preferences, it seems justifiable to conclude that at least a majority coalition of constituents favor some private provision of public goods and services in exchange for regulatory concessions.

Governmental regulation of private enterprise takes many forms, and there are many degrees of regulation. Therefore, it would be useful to try to identify which type of regulated firm is best suited to obtain remuneration through the compensatory relaxation of the regulatory constraints under which it operates in exchange for the public goods and services it supplies. The public utilities (electric, gas, and telephone services) are generally ideally suited for the receipt of such compensation. First, since the prices charged for their products are directly controlled through regulation, small incremental adjustments in the regulatory constraint (prices or rates), which are necessary in order to adequately control the compensation firms receive in exchange for supplying public goods, are easily affected. Also, each public utility firm can be treated independently with regard to adjustments in the regulatory constraint. This prevents those firms that do not supply sufficient quantities of public services from benefiting when a single regulatory constraint affecting all firms is incrementally relaxed because of the public service activities of a few firms.[13]

In addition, public utilities are usually identified with their local communities.[14, 15] This public image of the utility facilitates community acceptance of their role as a provider of public goods and services, which in turn enhances the likelihood that compensation would be rendered through a relaxation of regulatory constraints faced by the firm.

The metropolitan areawide service of many public utilities and their ability to charge different customers different rates provides them with

[13] For example, if the Civil Aeronautics Board increased airline fares to compensate for the public goods provided by one airline, the other airlines would benefit from the price rise, even though they may have supplied no public goods. This "free-rider" problem reduces the incentive for individual firms to provide public goods and services.

[14] See A. E. Kahn, *The Economics of Regulation: Principles and Institutions* (New York, Wiley, 1970) vol. I, p. 195; and Samuels, "Externalities," p. 394.

[15] In 1965, the electric utility industry consisted of 3,614 firms, of which approximately 3,000 were local distribution systems owned by municipalities or rural cooperatives. See Kahn, *The Economics of Regulation*, vol. II, p. 74.

a great deal of flexibility and a potentially broad revenue base upon which to draw for financing public goods and services for the metropolitan area as a whole, or for the central city alone. That is, if public utility rates are raised (relaxation of the regulatory constraint) to compensate the firm for supplying public services to the community, the cost could be spread over the entire metropolitan area through an incremental charge to all the customers of the utility, or it could be concentrated in certain areas or on certain groups.

Finally, the periodic utility commission rate hearings provide an open forum for the articulation of consumer preferences concerning the extent to which the firm should be allowed to recover the cost of supplying public goods and services through higher prices for its private products.

Given that public utility firms are well suited to the provision of public goods and services in exchange for regulatory concessions, and recalling from the empirical background material already presented that public utilities are actively engaged in providing these goods and services, a more formal model of a regulated firm engaged in these activities will be based on the general characteristics of the public utility firm.

The firm is represented in the model by a monopolist in the production of a single, private consumption good, designated X, whose price P is directly controlled by a regulatory agency operating under the sanction of politically elected officials (that is, a legislature or an elected chief executive). The firm is also assumed to be capable of supplying a public good G and will do so in exchange for permission to charge a sufficiently high price for X, since it is assumed that when no G is supplied by the firm, the regulated P is below the unconstrained profit-maximizing price.[16]

In actuality, public utility prices are determined through an adversary collective choice procedure known as *rate hearings*. The appropriate regulatory commission listens to proposals and arguments presented by the firm and consumers (or any other interested parties), and on the basis of the arguments and the evidence presented, determines the prices

---

[16] The pure public good referred to in the model is a commodity characterized by a prohibitively high cost of excluding additional individuals from consuming it, and a zero marginal cost of serving additional consumers. Examples of commodities with pure public good characteristics are national defense and radio or television signals transmitted through the air. Even though the commodity in the model is assumed to be purely public, all the results would hold for a commodity with private good characteristics as well.

to be charged. This is essentially a bargaining process, with the final outcome consisting of a price structure that favors the party with the greater relative bargaining strength. Along with the establishment of the basic rate structure, the bargaining process (rate hearing) also determines the extent to which the cost of public goods and services supplied by the regulated firm is permitted to be recovered through higher prices. Presumably, the regulatory agency will permit increases in the price of utility services to cover the cost of public goods and services supplied, so long as it is mutually beneficial to the firm (through higher profits) and to consumers (through increased welfare or utility).

Therefore, it is assumed that the underlying bargaining process operates in such a way as to result in the regulatory commission ultimately permitting a price P to be charged which allows the firm to recover the cost of supplying a corresponding quantity of G, which exhausts all mutual gains accruing to the firm and a majority coalition of consumers. That is, neither the firm nor any majority coalition of consumers could be made better off through a different combination of G and P without the other being made worse off.[17] This state is defined to be an equilibrium in the model.

EFFICIENCY

We now turn to a consideration of the impact which the private provision of public goods will have on the efficient utilization of society's resources.[18] It has been generally asserted that public utility pricing on a basis other than strict cost-of-service will generate inefficiencies through a distorted allocation of society's resources.[19] Clearly, the firm's provision of a public good that is financed by a higher price for its private

[17] This implicitly assumes that collective action is based on the aggregation of individual preferences (demand for G). Furthermore, it is assumed that majority rule governs the consumer input into the regulatory process. The rationale for this is that, presumably, a majority coalition of consumers could influence appropriate elected officials, who in turn have control over the regulatory agency through legislative authority and the power of appointment.

[18] The concept of efficiency used here is synonymous with the notion of Pareto optimality, which is defined to be an allocation of society's resources such that no individual could be made better off by any reallocation without any other individual being made worse off.

[19] See Bonbright, *Principles,* p. 116; and Samuels, "Externalities," p. 382.

product violates the strict cost-of-service pricing rule and is tantamount to imposing an excise tax on X in order to finance G.

The standard economic evaluation of an excise tax is that it produces an inefficient allocation of resources. It does so because the price of the taxed commodity distorts consumer choice between that commodity and other untaxed commodities relative to the choice among the commodities if their prices reflected only the true social opportunity cost of producing them. However, it has been demonstrated that in a world in which there are no distortion-free taxes (that is, a "second-best" world), a selective excise tax may be no more inefficient than any other type of tax employed to raise revenues.[20] This implies that in a world where there is no distortion-free governmental tax instrument used to finance the collective provision of public goods, the implicit excise tax method used to compensate regulated firms for supplying public goods is not necessarily any less efficient than alternative methods of providing these goods. In fact, the provision of public goods by the regulated firm can be consistent with a fully efficient ("first-best") allocation of resources, when the elasticity of demand for the firm's private product satisfies the following relationship:

(1) $$E = 1 + (MC_X/MC_G) \cdot R$$

where E is the elasticity of demand for X, MC_X is the marginal cost of producing X, MC_G is the marginal cost of producing G, and R is a measure of the degree to which X and G are complements or substitutes [that is, when R is greater (less) than 0, X and G are complements (substitutes)].[21] When the demand for the firm's private product is independent of the quantity of the public good being supplied, the complement–substitute coefficient R is equal to 0, and the firm can be expected to be fully efficient in supplying G only if the elasticity of demand for X is equal to 1. Moreover, when X and G are complements (substitutes), efficiency can be attained only when the elasticity of demand for X is greater (less) than 1 and satisfies equation 1.

---

[20] This proposition has been demonstrated in the literature addressing the second-best problem. See, for example, W. J. Baumol, and D. F. Bradford, "Optimal Departures from Marginal Cost Pricing," *American Economic Review* (June 1970) pp. 265–283.

[21] For the interested reader, a derivation of equation 1 is presented in the appendix to this chapter.

This relationship, expressed in equation 1, is important because it provides governmental units with the information necessary to ensure the most efficient supply of public goods possible. Armed with an estimate of the elasticity of demand for a regulated firm's private product, a measure of the degree of complementarity or substitutability between its private product and the public services it provides, and possessing schedules of the marginal cost of production for the public and private goods, the government can decide which regulated firms are the most efficient suppliers of public goods. This information could then be used to design public policies which would encourage those firms identified as efficient suppliers to continue their activities, while discouraging the inefficient firms, through appropriate regulatory incentives and controls. This identification and selection process would have the additional effect of stimulating the regulated firms to choose a public goods mix that has the degree of complementarity or substitutability with its jointly produced private product, and the relative marginal cost structure, which comes closest to being fully efficient for a given elasticity of demand for the private good.

DISTRIBUTIONAL EFFECTS

Under a system where majority rule prevails in the collective choice process, and consequently, indirectly determines regulatory agency decisions, there may be a tendency for regulated firms to choose to provide public goods whose benefits are conferred only upon a majority coalition of consumers. This would be done because the firm needs only to satisfy a majority constituency in order to win the approval of a politically sensitive regulatory agency. However, efficiency in the private supply of public goods can only be achieved if the benefits accrue to all consumers who bear the cost. This requirement is necessary because the concept of economic efficiency in the provision of public goods corresponds to the maximization of the total of individual net benefits (total individual benefits minus total costs). Consequently, in situations where a majority coalition receives all the benefits but does not bear all the costs, there is an incentive for them to demand more than the efficient level of the public good. This is not to say that regulated firms should not provide public services that benefit only a subset of the consumers of their private product; but it does imply that, in order to avoid unnecessary resource allocation distortions, only the subset who benefits from the public good should have to bear the cost of the service through higher prices for the private good.

Due to the nature of the public utility price structure, it is possible to charge different rates for different consumer groups, and this is presently done. Within limits, this flexibility in pricing permits the cost burden of public services to be distributed in a manner deemed equitable by society. The limitations imposed on this flexibility depend upon the ability of the equitably chosen price structure to generate sufficient revenue to induce the firm to supply these services—the price elasticity of demand for the firm's private product, associated with different consumer groups, may not be appropriate for raising the needed revenue when rates are raised in an equitable fashion.

On the benefit side, the attainment of collectively determined distributional goals may be further enhanced when regulated firms supply public goods whose benefits are not necessarily conferred evenly on all consumers of the firm's private product. The public good may be chosen so that the largest portion of benefits accrue to a specified subset of consumers, while the cost can be spread over all, or some other subset, of the firm's consumers through selectively higher prices.

It should be noted that in a world where there are no allocationally neutral tax or transfer instruments, it will not generally be possible to satisfy both the equity and efficiency criteria, and the collective choice process will determine the tradeoff between these two standards.

CONCLUSIONS

At the present time, only a very small portion of the excess demand for public goods and services in local areas is being supplied by regulated firms under the guise of the social responsibility of business or corporate philanthropy. However, due to a changing public attitude toward business activity, the provision of public goods by regulated firms is growing, and can reasonably be expected to reach significant proportions in the future. If the regulated firm is compensated for these activities by the relaxation of the constraints under which the firm operates, and if the model developed above accurately represents the firms involved in these activities, then the analysis demonstrates that the private provision of public goods and services through the regulated firm need not result in an inefficient allocation of society's resources nor an inequitable distribution of the costs and benefits of these activities. However, the extent to which the mix of efficiency and equity standards desired by the community is actually fulfilled in the private provision of public goods and services depends critically on the efficacy of the collective choice process. It is through the collective choice mechanism that individual consumer preferences for public goods and services are translated into operational policy decisions of the regulatory commissions and other government agencies which control the compensation the firm receives for providing these services. Therefore, the more effective the collective choice mechanism is in performing its function, the more effective the private provision of public services will be in satisfying the preferences of the community.

In the final analysis, then, the critical policy issue concerns whether private firms should be discouraged from pursuing public service activities. The answer depends upon whether the collective choice process is any more effective in satisfying the public service demands of individual consumers through traditional government provision than it is in controlling the compensation received by private firms that voluntarily supply similar goods and services. Unfortunately, this issue can only be resolved with a better understanding of the processes and institutions through which collective choices are made, and this is an important area for further research.

APPENDIX A: DERIVATION OF THE RELATIONSHIP BETWEEN ECONOMIC EFFICIENCY AND THE ELASTICITY OF DEMAND FOR X (EQUATION 1)

Assume that there is a single consumer with a utility function,

(A-1) $$U = U(X(P), G)$$

where $X(P)$ is the consumer's demand function for X.[22] The profit function for a monopolistic firm whose price is regulated is,

(A-2) $$\pi = P \cdot X(P) - C(X(P), G)$$

[22] For a more extensive development of the underlying model upon which the derivation is based, and for a generalization to more than one consumer under majority rule, see J. M. Cummins, *Public Goods, Collective Choice, and the Regulated Firm* (Stanford, Calif., Stanford University Graduate School of Business, August 1975) research paper no. 272.

where π equals firm profits and $C(X(P),G)$ is the total cost function for the firm, which depends on the level of X and G produced. The public good G only directly influences the firm's profits through the cost function but has an indirect impact on revenue when the regulated price P is increased to compensate the firm for supplying G.

An equilibrium is defined in the model as a state where all gains from trade between the firm and the consumer are exhausted with respect to the exchange of G for compensating increases in P. Assuming that the consumer maximizes utility and the firm maximizes profits, attainment of an interior equilibrium implies a tangency between a representative consumer indifference curve and an iso-profit curve for the firm.

The equilibrium condition can be derived by equating the slope of an iso-profit curve with the slope of an indifference curve. The slope of the iso-profit curve is obtained by totally differentiating the profit function with respect to variations in P and G, setting the result equal to 0, and and then solving for dP/dG. That is,

(A-3) $d\pi = [(MR - MC_X)\partial X/\partial P]\cdot dP + [(P - MC_X)\partial X/\partial G - MC_G]\cdot dG$

$= 0$

where MR equals marginal revenue, and $\partial X/\partial G$ is a measure of the degree of complementarity or substitutability between X and G (the term R in equation 1, on page 138). Solving equation A-3 for the slope gives,

(A-4) $dP/dG = \dfrac{-(P - MC_X)\partial X/\partial G - MC_G}{(MR - MC_X)\partial X/\partial P}$

The slope of the indifference curve is derived in a similar manner:

(A-5) $dU = [\partial U/\partial X \cdot \partial X/\partial P]\cdot dP + [\partial U/\partial X \cdot \partial X/\partial G + \partial U/\partial G]\cdot dG = 0$

Solving for the slope and collecting terms yields,

(A-6) $dP/dG = -\left(\partial X/\partial G + \dfrac{\partial U/\partial G}{\partial U/\partial X}\right) \cdot \dfrac{1}{\partial X/\partial P}$

where the ratio of the marginal utility of G to the marginal utility of X is the familiar marginal rate of substitution between the two goods (designated as MRS).

The equilibrium condition is obtained by equating A-4 and A-6. Thus,

(A-7) $\dfrac{(P - MC_X)\partial X/\partial G - MC_G}{MR - MC_X} = \partial X/\partial G + MRS$

Solving for MRS, and obtaining a common denominator for the other side of the equation yields,

$$(A\text{-}8) \quad MRS = \frac{(P - MC_X)\partial X/\partial G - MC_G - (MR - MC_X)\partial X/\partial G}{MR - MC_X}$$

When $P - (P/E)$ is substituted for MR, in equation A-8, from the standard relationship between marginal revenue and the elasticity of demand, then the equilibrium relationship reduces to,

$$(A\text{-}9) \quad MRS = \frac{(P/E)\partial X/\partial G - MC_G}{P - (P/E) - MC_X}$$

The well-known necessary condition for efficiency in the provision of a public good is that the sum over all consumers of the marginal rate of substitution between G and X must equal the marginal rate of transformation between the public and the private good. In a one-consumer model, this efficiency condition becomes, $MRS = MC_G/MC_X$.

To ensure that the equilibrium in the model satisfies the efficiency requirement, the right-hand side of equation A-9 must be equal to the marginal rate of transformation between G and X:

$$(A\text{-}10) \quad \frac{(P/E)\partial X/\partial G - MC_G}{P - (P/E) - MC_X} = MC_G/MC_X$$

Multiplying both sides of equation A-10 by $P - (P/E) - MC_X$ and MC_X/MC_G, and then collecting terms gives,

$$(A\text{-}11) \quad (MC_X/MC_G)\cdot(P/E)\cdot\partial X/\partial G = P - (P/E)$$

Finally, multiplying both sides of equation A-11 by E/P, and then solving for E yields,

$$(A\text{-}12) \quad E = 1 + (MC_X/MC_G)\cdot\partial X/\partial G$$

Equation A-12 is identical with equation 1 (on page 138), when $\partial X/\partial G$ is represented by R, and this establishes the relationship between economic efficiency in the private provision of G and the elasticity of demand for X.